Hire for Fit

HERE'S WHAT PEOPLE ARE SAYING ABOUT
HIRE FOR FIT

Hire for Fit is a must read for both employers and job seekers. In today's volatile job market, it's critically important that there is a focus on fitting a company's culture and that tough questions be asked during the interview process. *Hire for Fit* offers all the right advice.

—James A. Kaitz
President and CEO
Association for Financial Professionals

Hire for Fit is an outstanding resource everyone with hiring responsibilities up to the CEO and Board of Directors level must read to avoid the millions of annual dollars lost due to bad hires.

—John Antonio Negroni
Conference Program Director
The Conference Board

Hire for Fit is a great practical guide for managers who hire people. The issues presented are real and the suggestions are applicable and concise.

—Albert Siu
Vice President, Human Resources
Education and Training
AT&T

In addition to being well written and concise, *Hire for Fit* develops in clear terms this most important issue "fit" in the hiring process. Hopefully the participants on all sides of the equation will learn from this book and demand the focus essential to these long-term employment relationships that everyone desires.

—Matthew R. Bud
Chairman
The Financial Executives Consulting Group

Hire for Fit provides practical, antidotal steps to solve the continual dilemma of finding the best round peg for the most important round hole. Its **PRODUCTIVE ENTRANCE STRATEGY**® is a clear indication of a well thought-out approach to smooth the hiring process.

—Victor M. Richel
Vice-Chairman
Independence Community Bank

Today's workplace has changed and it will never be the same. The process of hiring a manager, executive, and/or leader is complex and can be costly if certain guidelines are not followed. *Hire for Fit* clearly addresses the process of hiring right the first time and provides what people need to know and what they need to do in order to put the right person in the right position with the right job description for success within any organization.

Hire for Fit must become required reading for those involved in the hiring process as well as those people in transition that are looking for a position that best utilizes their skills and experience. It will save companies time, energy, and money (literally in the millions) and reduce the impact of token relationships in the workplace.

—Mark LeBlanc
President
Small Business Success

When I think of the costs of mis-hiring, it's enormous. This book is a blessing.

—Christine Harvey
Author, *Secrets of World's Top Sales Performers*
Past Chair—London Chamber of Commerce

Select
the Best
Executive
for Your
Organization

HIRE FOR FIT

Don Andersson

OAKHILL PRESS
Winchester, Virginia

10   9   8   7   6   5   4   3   2   1

Library of Congress Cataloging-in-Publication Data

Andersson, Don
    Hire for fit : select the best executive for your organization / Don Andersson
      p. cm.
    Includes index.
    ISBN 1-886939-45-4 (alk. paper)
    1. Executives—Recruiting. 2. Executives—Selection and appointment. 3. Executives—Training of. 4. Executive Ability. I. Title.

HF5549.5.R44 A53 2000
658.4'0711--dc21

                              00-047859

Oakhill Press
461 Layside Drive
Winchester, VA 22602
800-32-BOOKS
Printed in the United States of America

In Appreciation

Alertness to the most needy, an instinctive determination to quietly be responsive to them and a cheerful accountability to a greater good than self-interest—these are the threads from which the legacy influencing my life has been fashioned.

Countless examples of those who have added extra richness come easily to mind. I am thankful for the contribution of each and especially for those who were the primary fashioners of the inheritance of values entrusted to me. It is to them—my mother and father—this book is affectionately dedicated.

Lillian Covey-Frank

Floyd August Andersson

Contents

CONTENTS

Part IV: Support Success

THE PRODUCTIVE ENTRANCE STRATEGY®

Acknowledgements

Those who have gone before us have had a major impact in shaping the present in which we find ourselves. As inheritors of their legacy, you and I have the opportunity of pruning, extending, and developing it whenever we place our own unique imprint upon it.

The insights you may receive by reading your way through this book are intended to function in the same way. Through the wisdom, experience, and expertise of many, I've had the opportunity to learn much. I've also had the opportunity to use that knowledge to open additional doors and windows that have expanded my understanding. I'm hopeful you'll do the same with the information you gather here.

Use your personal insight-inheritance as a basis to extend and develop your future. As you do, I would welcome an opportunity to learn from your applications.

There are so many from whom I've had the opportunity to learn and for whom I give thanks.

To John C. Talbot, who first invited me to investigate and begin understanding the world of organizational development—thanks!

To my colleagues of the National Speakers Association and especially to the members of the Tri-State

Chapter who have always been available and ready to let me benefit from their insights—thanks!

To those who have trusted me with their fears, frustrations, failures and hopes—and in so doing have become significant co-authors of this book—thanks!

To members of the Financial Executive Networking Group who have provided me with a forum in which to write and receive feedback as their Transition Coach—thanks!

To those executives I've met along the Transition Highway—in response to a presentation I've made, an article I've written, or to something they've noticed on my web site and who have raised questions that have led to yet more facets for my learning—thanks!

To Barbara McNichol, my editor, who brought understanding, affirmation and an ability to sharpen my focus as she collaborated with me in shaping this manuscript—thanks!

To Ed Helvey, Paula Gould and the remainder of the Oakhill Press team for their expertise and always good-natured cooperation in helping my thoughts become this reality—thanks!

To those colleagues who shared their time with and for me by reading my manuscript and who, in comments drawn upon their diversity of experience, helped me to strengthen its content. I want to especially thank Toni Boyle, Matt Bud, Rick Jakle, Jim Kaitz, Mike Kent, Mark LeBlanc, Paul Litwack, Paul Mayer, John Negroni, Anne O'Herron, Guy Pedilini, Vic Richel, Albert Siu, and Barbara-Lynn Taylor.

To John Negroni, Rick Shapiro, and Barbara-Lynn Taylor—yes I know I've mentioned a couple of them above—but I wanted to single these three out even more for their constant support and for the growing friendship I have with each of them. They are each very special to me.

To my daughters Maura, Greta, Sara-Britt and Katrina whose maturing has been a constant catalyst prodding me to continue my own growth and immeasurably helping me to expand my appreciation of differences—thanks for being the very unique individuals you are becoming.

Lastly and most importantly, my special thanks to Judy. Sharing the challenges and joys of life with me, patiently dealing with my idiosyncrasies that are even more magnified whenever I write, always there to help—you are the model of goodness and I am so glad you are in my life.

Never do we create out of nothing. To grasp hold of the many threads of life that are presented to us— as welcomed or unwelcomed gifts from others—

and from them to weave a tapestry that bears our special imprint—that is the opportunity each of us has been given.

May we continue to value and learn from the insights of each other and may we add to them for the good of us all.

Introduction— HELP!

"I'm really at a loss," said the vice president of human resources. "We've done a tough piece of work merging three companies.

"We've let people go, shifted positions, and made selective hires. One of the best jobs we've done has been with Information Systems—at least that's what I thought.

"Everyone has been working out fine . . . a creative team, pulling together. But now they're ready to revolt . . . to leave practically en masse as soon as they collect their bonuses.

"We've got a mess and it began when we hired our CIO. Technically he's a genius, but he's not working out—isn't getting along with people. I need help. What can I do with someone who just doesn't fit?"

Across the corporate landscape, similar scenes play out daily. Individuals with great expertise and résumés reflecting outstanding experience impress interviewers who extend an offer that's quickly accepted. As earnest as they may be, however, there is no guarantee that those who have been able to shine brightly in one place will be able to glitter in yours.

Low unemployment rates do not nullify the reality of frequent transition. Whether it's described as "irreconcilable differences" or, more euphemistically, as a desire to "pursue other opportunities," the costly turnover of executives continues. Current studies indicate that, on average, today's executive will hold eight to ten different positions throughout her or his career—and the cost of each transition can run up to *24 times* that person's base salary.

Some of that transition is rightly attributed to the ripple effect of mergers and acquisitions with their subsequent shifts in leadership. As the technological revolution continues, some executives fail to remain "state of the art" with their technical skills. More won't make it because they are unable to successfully contribute within the milieu of a particular organization.

Organizations differ. Some are highly transactional. Some are deliberative. Some are hierarchical. Some are collaborative. Each has its own unique stream of priorities.

None of these factors is implicitly wrong. However, each requires unique and different skills that should be given significance in your selection process. If neglected, your selection process can drift into an unintended collusion to fail, not because technical skills are missing but because the chosen candidate just doesn't possess the ability to work productively in your particular work context.

Your partnership contribution

Neither those doing the selecting nor the ones chosen want to experience failure—quite the contrary—but there's no guarantee of success. Improved results, however, can be attained through a partnership effort between organizational leaders and executive candidates who pay close attention to the critical success factors explained in the chapters that follow.

Corporate and association leaders who want to hire for a world-class organization will benefit from *Hire for Fit*. So will every other manager who is involved in choosing a new executive and who wants that individual to get a quick start. Those who are currently going through transition or who have just landed will also discover critical insights into what they must *know* and what they must *do* to be successful. This book is a must for every manager at every level!

In its five major sections, it focuses on the initiatives that position a new executive for success. It recognizes the contextual reality of the hiring process, pushes leaders toward an awareness of what else is required, invites them to take action, and encourages them to recognize their role in supporting the newly hired in making a productive entrance. And, it provides a tested resource that can be put to immediate use.

What you've inherited

Lack of clear definition can cause a well-intentioned executive to fail, affecting your organization with the very high cost and ripple effect of turnover. It's the legacy resulting from these key factors:

- failing to view vacancies as opportunities to leverage your organization's potential for success

- working from outdated position descriptions

- ignoring the necessary factors that contribute to fitting into your unique work environment.

It's easy to continue plodding on in existing patterns until you're stuck in a rut—and to forget that the only difference between a rut and a grave is its depth. In today's climate in which organizations scramble to survive first and succeed next, it's understandable to ask, "Who has the time to develop and use a different selection template and process?" It's possible that the even more critical question to ask is, "How willing am I to change the process so we can all succeed?"

Growing awareness

Position descriptions that list responsibilities, experience, and technical expertise can sound helpful and complete, even when information essential to appropriate selection is missing. Inevitably overlooked is any significant consideration of the context in which one is to succeed—and that makes a big difference!

To complement technically oriented position descriptions, those conducting interviews need to be clear about how the position contributes to meeting overall goals. They need to be aware of factors uniquely influencing the work environment within your organization. Because diverse, nonprioritized, and unclear expectations can also impede success, they must be refined and reflected in the interviewing process.

Here is where what I refer to as "fit factors" enter in. These are the unique, interpersonal, and team—in addition to technical—skills that one must possess if she or he is to be able to productively contribute within the special nuances of your organization.

If you do not focus on these "fit factors," then assumptions—with all their complications—will reign and eventually create chaos. Fit matters— so pay attention to it!

Invitation to action

Selecting an executive is a courting process that attempts to determine the potential viability of a possible relationship. Impacted by an ever-changing work environment, that courtship has undergone tremendous alteration during the past few years. The pace of change continues to escalate. As individuals get a smattering of different experiences, for example, loyalty to the employer becomes a relic of the past. Turnover is frequent. And a technological knowledge explosion accompanying an emerging "dot com" world means that now—more than ever—insights from others are critical to success.

In practical terms, that means there's a need for a customer-responsive position description and a new criterion for success—one recognizing that technical capabilities aren't enough. One must also identify and search for specific soft skills—both interpersonal and team—that a candidate needs to be effective.

Remember that selection remains a partnership event. As is true with all relationships, neither party will completely fill the other's wants— there must be give and take. Establishing a range of desires for both parties has to be present to successfully hire for fit.

Support success

Despite her or his competence, every newly hired executive needs help to understand what's unique about your organization and to be clear about the diverse expectations that others have. To assume differently is to impede that person's ability to make a quick and productive entrance.

Specifically, newly-hired executives need precisely what they *can't* provide for themselves. From your organization, they need:

- clarity in understanding what needs to be accomplished

- knowledge of how success will be measured

- details about what contribution they are expected to make

- someone to point out how organizational currents and undercurrents flow

They also need:

- a readiness to affirmatively respond to the opportunities revealed by their fresh perspective

- work relationships that are consistent and well defined

- resources to implement their initiatives

THE PRODUCTIVE ENTRANCE STRATEGY®

This concluding resource puts it all together and gets you started with specific action items in a user-friendly format. As one dot com executive has stated, "'**THE PRODUCTIVE ENTRANCE STRATEGY®**, A Resource for Success,' has synthesized everything we have known, suspected, wondered about, and ignored into an easy-to-follow guide to hiring the right person."

If you implement the ideas in this book and use **THE PRODUCTIVE ENTRANCE STRATEGY®** resource in chapter 24 consistently, you will no longer place square pegs in round holes. Instead, you will be laying the groundwork for hiring the best person for your organization.

A personal note

A decade ago, when I first began specializing in executive transition, I believed that whenever entry failure occurred, it was the candidate's fault. That tenet was supported by candidates who blamed themselves for failure and by organizational leaders who sincerely believed the salaries they paid absolved them from the need to support success.

As I've coached both sets of individuals over the years, I've come to realize that a successful selection and start-up depends on both. If the potential opportunities inherent in filling a vacancy are to be leveraged, both partners must take responsibility.

In one way or another, everyone with whom I've worked has been my teacher. They often had no idea how influential they were. In sharing their vulnerabilities and their fears, joys, hopes, frustrations, failures, and successes, they have paved the way to new insights for me.

I've quoted many of them without attaching any names. As long as they've learned from their efforts, have taught others, and provided me with a story to share, what difference does it make? Truth is always truth, no matter who said it.

I appreciate the opportunity to be a resource for you and welcome any feedback you might care to provide.

PART I
What You've Inherited

CHAPTER 1

Uncle Louie, Blanche, and Sylvia

"I am really ticked off," said a vice president of marketing, two weeks into his new position. "We're running very lean—stretched about as much as we can be. I'm expected to get a pile of work done in a hurry with limited resources—and I've been told I can't ask for more staff.

"Just before I got here, they hired Sylvia as my administrative assistant. She's got the social graces of a barracuda. She doesn't have sufficient computer skills and could care less. I'm stuck with her.

"She got fired from her last position . . . but Sylvia is the daughter of my boss's current girlfriend. He watches out for her and won't talk to me about the situation."

It could be the boss's girlfriend's daughter Sylvia or someone's Uncle Louie or Aunt Blanche who needed a job. The private—as well as the public— sector has its patronage system in which people get hired just because of whom they know.

"I think Louie is the VP's uncle. He's been rotating between jobs for quite a while—at least that's what the rumor mill says. He's a bit rough around the edges. He tries to make a good impression but no one seems to know what he's supposed to be doing—even him. It looks like he's being paid to be parked in place until they find out how they're going to use him. While he sits and waits, the rest of us are really swamped. It's certainly not helpful for morale. Connections can really be important, can't they?"

"I'd like to know how we got the privilege of having Blanche in our department. She's got her own office but in the three weeks she's been 'working,' the most she's said to anyone is 'good morning.' She spends a lot of time on the phone. Whom she talks to or why she's talking to them remains a mystery. She seems to exist in her own world. It sure would be nice if someone told us what her job was."

That's reality! At times, we've all worked with certain people and wondered how they ever managed to land the jobs they had. Often they're assigned to "special projects" that may have importance. Observers, however, can easily assume they're involved in make-work and are protected by someone in a high place.

In these increasingly competitive times there's been a shift. People are still being hired because of whom they know—although fewer and fewer get their positions just because they're someone's uncle, aunt, or girlfriend's daughter.

What's new?

In today's marketplace, with its emphasis on networking, it's becoming more common to use connections as a way of identifying potential opportunities. Groups of executives in transition are constantly being used to learn what's happening on the street, to identify vacancies, to gather background information, and to conduct due diligence. They're also being used to identify key contacts who can provide access to candidates for consideration.

Leaders in organizations are also encouraging their executives to network by leveraging external business relationships. They want them to constantly stay alert to new industry "stars" who might be lured into a change of venue. Successful recruitment may even result in a bonus for the one who suggested and "landed" the new hire.

"There are some really good people out there who could help us," CEOs have been saying. "We need to keep our eyes open for them. Some of our vendors may even be aware of executives working for our competitors. They can be open to our efforts if we play our cards right. That way, we might be able to avoid some of the hassles associated with the traditional search process."

Is this new way better?

Superficial screening by colleagues provides no assurance that the contributions of those referred will be any better than those of Uncle Louie, Blanche, or Sylvia. Their capabilities may still not be the right ones for your organization. The range of technical, interpersonal, and team skills your company needs to be competitive may still be missing.

Remember, success in another organization does not guarantee success in yours! Organizations differ and so does what it takes to work effectively within them. Your executive candidate may have the technical skills your organization desperately needs yet still not have what it takes to "fit."

"Technically I couldn't ask for anyone better," said a CEO, referring to his information officer. "If we have a systems problem, he knows how to fix it— and he does—quickly!

"But I need someone with more than technical know-how. We're growing fast and we need to be responsive to the expanding demands of our people. That takes face-to-face contact and he just can't pull that off. He has a hard time communicating and he gives everybody the impression he doesn't know how to listen.

"I've got to let him go and find someone who can be more helpful."

▲▼▲▼

Today's search for talent is never ending. There are, or will be, vacancies to fill. There are, and will continue to be, individuals searching for new opportunities—but that's not enough. Success depends upon an appropriate match between an individual and a position.

In making referrals, most people want to be helpful matchmakers—but helpful to *whom*? Are they trying to help the potential candidate because they really believe the "fit" is appropriate? Are they trying to help your organization first and foremost? Do they know exactly what your company is looking for? Do *you*?

The issue isn't whether you can get candidates to consider, it's this—since square pegs don't make it in round holes, do those candidates you are considering have what it takes to "fit"?

CHAPTER

2

It's Not Just a Résumé You're Hiring

Beatrice was young, star-bright, on the cutting edge of technology—and she worked for the competition. Those within the organization were very aware of her reputation. With the proverbial sack of gold, they enticed her away and positioned her as second-in-command of a division.

The day she began work, the division president left her in charge and flew to Russia for a three-week business trip. When he checked into his Moscow hotel, a message awaited. "Please call your office immediately." He responded and received an earful.

"You can't believe what Beatrice is doing. She's turning this place upside down. She's starting to change everything. She's acting without asking any questions. She doesn't understand what we are trying to do. She doesn't seem to realize that it's better to have friends than enemies."

His instinctive reaction was to placate. "Things will get better. All she needs is some time," he told them. But additional calls of frustration came on day two. Day three produced even more intense and angry feedback, forcing him to realize it would be better to cancel the remainder of his trip and return to take care of business in his office.

He discovered his division had quickly degenerated into shambles. Upset reigned! No one was focused on getting the job done. They were focused on Beatrice—and Beatrice didn't have a clue! Even when pressed, she could not comprehend the ripple effect her "few little suggestions" had created.

Within six weeks of starting with the corporation, she was asked to leave it. Her up-until-then brilliant professional ascent had been at least temporarily derailed. Those who had selected her faced the ugly aftermath of a bad decision. Their selection was under postmortem scrutiny. Many whispered quiet judgments. Anger lingered. Multiple wounds needed to heal. Productivity waned. Deadlines and new opportunities continued to be missed. That's not what the company needed and it's certainly not what Beatrice wanted to happen.

Frequency of short-termers

Becoming a short-term employment statistic happens frequently. Recent studies indicate that within eighteen to twenty-four months, up to 40 percent of all executives entering new positions will either leave voluntarily, be terminated, or receive an unsatisfactory performance review. Other studies conclude that today's average length of stay in an executive position is less than four years—and it's getting shorter.

Sometimes it's because corporate direction took a major shift. Sometimes it's because the leadership changed. More often it's because those who did the interviewing focused primarily on a candidate's *technical* skills necessary to address operational needs. Most likely they completely ignored the *people* skills essential for success. They may never have asked themselves if the candidate would be the right "fit."

"I lasted about eight months," Bill said. "I was brought into a growing family-owned business to be the chief financial officer. Quite honestly, things were a mess . . . but I took charge. I did a good cash-flow analysis, spoke with vendors and customers, reviewed past spending patterns, and developed a plan of action. Then I listened to the sales force.

"They breathed a sigh of relief when I just listened to them and began to provide some direction. They told me that's the kind of support they needed but were not getting from members of the family.

"From a business perspective, things began to turn around. In just a few months, we saw a positive impact. I proved to myself that I was capable of making a major contribution.

"But I screwed up. I didn't take the time to build relationships with the family members. My plan was working but, because I hadn't involved them in it, they didn't feel committed to it. I just assumed that all that mattered was getting results. Looking back, I know I overlooked a critical step. They needed to feel included, and when they didn't, they took it out on me.

"I guess I just broke the mold of the way they were used to working. I didn't fit so they asked me

to leave. I've got to be very careful about that the
next time. I never realized how important it is to fit
if I'm going to be successful."

High-profile senior executives often fall into a similar trap. Operationally they could be getting results, but their independent actions may undercut any possibility of support. They're so busy getting things done that they make no effort to fit. That's extracting an unacceptable price.

Monitor the Who's News section of the *Wall Street Journal* for a month and note how many executives leave after a relatively short time to "pursue other interests." Recognize that's only a tiny tip of reality peeking through.

Some executive departures get more splashy coverage. When Michael Ovitz left Disney, he recognized that issues other than his skills caused his early demise. "I made the biggest mistake of my business career," he told E!Online. "It was a stupid idea that I could change this culture."

John R. Walter, once scheduled to become CEO at AT&T, was denied that post. He had initially been chosen because of his success in guiding the printing company R.R. Donnelley and Sons into the technology age. Wall Street analysts and other CEOs, however, soon branded him as a telecommunications industry outsider who just didn't fit.

Philip Pfeffer, longtime book industry executive,

left as the CEO of Borders Group Inc. after little more than five months. Board chairman Robert DiRomualdo stated, "All I can say is that it just wasn't a good fit and we want to move on."

When I left my position as a CEO and returned to working with a variety of management teams, I was surprised to recognize how rampant turnover was even at senior levels of an organization. Despite today's high employment rate, the pace continues to quicken. It's becoming increasingly accurate to say that every professional is in transition these days. It's only a matter of time.

▲▼▲▼

Candidates are repeatedly selected based on a résumé, comments from references, and assessments (*often unfocused and uncoordinated*) made by those looking for someone who has the technical competence and experience to do the job. Rarely, however, is the *ability to fit* given serious consideration.

Despite everyone's good intentions, that overlooking of fit frequently involves interviewers, company decision makers, and the newly hired executive. It's a reality that can easily lead to an unrecognized and undesired *collusion to fail*.

Most people fail—not because they lack the required technical aptitudes, but because they don't fit!

Failure Ain't Cheap

"It really cost us," said a chairman of the board speaking of the recent termination of his CEO. "We thought he was the right choice or we wouldn't have made him an offer.

"We were wrong! He was a walking disaster. No people skills . . . on a power trip . . . hired his son into a high-paying position for which he was ill prepared . . . left wreckage wherever he went.

"We had to pay him $7.5 million to go bye-bye, and now we've got to go through the process all over again."

There are many high-profile examples. When Michael Ovitz left his post as president of Walt Disney Company after fourteen months, his severance totaled an estimated $90 million in cash and stock options. John R. Walter was selected to be the next-in-line CEO of AT&T and, in nine months, was pushed out with a reported severance package of $25 million. After a year and a half, the board of Apple Computer Inc. eased Gilbert F. Amelio from his chairman and CEO position for a reported $9.2 million.

Similar examples can be found in a number of organizations. Fingers are pointed but rarely at those who developed the position description or conducted the interviews. After all, they did what was asked. They looked for someone who had the requisite experience and technical skills to do the job—and found that person.

> "He couldn't get with the program. It's not our fault! We used the description they gave us. What fault is it of ours if the one we selected just wasn't able to do what they said they wanted? Now, in so many ways we're paying the price for it—and what a price!"

Failure ain't cheap!

Especially when there's an unexpected churn at the top of a publicly listed corporation, a ripple throughout the marketplace is inevitable. Even when anticipated, reassessments of an organization's viability automatically occur. Stock prices can take a hit.

Failure ain't cheap!

It's been estimated that the turnover costs of an average MBA just getting started will be at least 150 percent of the initial base salary. Move into higher levels and costs escalate.

In their book *Top Grading*, Geoff Smart and Bradford D. Smart conclude that "with an average base salary of $114,000, the average total costs associated with 'typical' mis-hires [is] $2,709,000—about 24 times the person's base compensation."

My own experience suggests that, by the time all costs are calculated, the average price of replacing a senior-level executive will fall between $1 and $10-plus million dollars—and may even be higher.

Failure ain't cheap!

Unfortunately, there's never a tabula rasa upon which to commence a new search precipitated when someone is asked to leave. There are always wounds that need to be healed, adding to the cost. During a period when positions are vacant, egos are bruised, productivity disrupted, and opportunities are lost! Those who worked for the one dismissed may flounder in their roles. Trust and confidence in the executives who were involved in the original selection that went astray are eroded! These costs are just as real as they are difficult to quantify.

Failure ain't cheap!

Other costs can be tabulated. If it's been more than six months since the mis-hire, there's apt to be a repeated recruiter cost. Expenses may be incurred to reexamine the process and perhaps rework the position description although my hunch—based on experience—is that little is apt to be done to redefine requirements.

> "No candidate we've presented has been acceptable," commented one recruiter for a major search firm. "We've repeatedly asked the decision maker to sit down with us and rework the specs.
>
> "We get cooperation from HR, but those who are critical to the final selection won't get involved. They say they just don't have time. Meanwhile, they're frustrated, we're frustrated and the clock keeps ticking. That's costly."

There's also the cost of identifying, transporting, and interviewing candidates—again. Factor in the time involved by internal gatekeepers who must repeat the process—only this time with even less enthusiasm—and the costs continue to mount.

Failure ain't cheap!

After the final selection, still more costs accrue. Given today's skittish marketplace realities, skills in short supply provide an opportunity for the incoming candidate to leverage perks. Signing bonuses—at least for senior executives—are becoming almost as common as they are for professional ball players. Stock options are used to entice. Vesting time is shortened. If relocation is necessary –and it frequently is– costs may include not only short-term housing that can last up to a year, but also the corporation's purchase of a house left behind.

When the new executive begins to discover what she or he has inherited, there's apt to be a ripple effect. Often current team members are evaluated and are dismissed or decide to leave. That brain drain of creativity, insight, and customer relations can be costly . . . and so can the price of handling the replacement.

▲▼▲▼

It's not just the obvious costs that ring up the price of mis-hires. It's the hidden ones set off by a variety of ripple effects. It costs to *not* be clear about the objective of your search. However well intentioned, it costs to clean up a mess that's been left behind. It costs to heal shattered relationships and reestablish equilibrium. One can only wonder about the cost of the opportunities once available—now, gone forever.

Since no resolution of past issues is completed by day one of the new hire, costs will continue to mount. They will include the price extracted by a learning curve that must be surmounted. They may also include the loss of employees not valued by the new executive as well as costs—almost always higher—for their replacements.

Failure ain't cheap—and it costs even more if you fail to learn from it!

The "Just Do It" Fallacy

"I need a new chief financial officer," the division president of a *Fortune* 500 company stated to his vice president of human resources. "Please get me one."

When more detailed information was requested, the division president responded,

"I don't have time to waste on developing a job description—that's your responsibility. You should have one on file. Print it out for me. Change it if you think it needs to be changed. Then give it to me to sign. Let's get this out to search as fast as we can. Just do it!"

To act as if a generic description will provide adequate guidance to select a candidate who can effectively contribute to your organization's success is faulty. To believe that someone else knows what capabilities you need in a person who directly reports to you is just as questionable. You cannot realistically rely on others to establish parameters of the path you want taken in the search unless you have been very clear about:

- the focus of your initiatives,

- the contributions you expect that position to make toward implementing those initiatives,

- the work environment you strive to create,

- the personal attributes you desire and that are needed to fit in your organization.

Being clear

If *you* aren't clear what you're looking for, how is it possible for anyone else—even the most brilliant and well-intentioned human resources professional—to be of assistance? Others have a critical role to play in interviewing and contributing to the viability assessment of candidates but, quite honestly, it's not their job to establish the overall picture. To expect that is to renege on your responsibility. How can they know what you don't? It's difficult to read what's on your mind if nothing is.

"If I'm going to really get my job done," said one CEO, "I've got to keep my people focused. I think that's the most critical thing I have to do—to help them understand what we're all about, and to keep repeating it over and over and over again. That's what it takes.

"It's so easy to get caught up in daily activities and forget why we're doing them. Every time we meet, I review again where we're headed and what we need to do to get there. I don't think that focus can be repeated enough. Those parameters—which it's my responsibility to establish—provide the guidance they need to make all kinds of operational decisions—from developing new marketing programs to selecting new personnel.

"If I can't get this people thing right, no matter how strong we are technically, we're never going to hit our potential. That's my job—to leverage our assets, beginning with our human capital."

Scrambling for talent

Today's marketplace is hectic. The pressure of time is constant and so is the scramble for talent that's often in short supply.

> "We've just signed a huge contract," said the head of a major engineering and construction firm. "We need at least 150 engineers and so far we've only been able to locate 93.
>
> "I'm afraid the shortage will soon force us to scrape the bottom of the barrel. We'll have to bring on some individuals who normally wouldn't even get a second look."

There are slots to be filled, and the sooner the better. That fast-paced, just-do-it focus breeds urgency. Even those who might prefer a more studied approach to screening and selection are often forced to conclude:

> "We just don't have the time."

> "We have more important things to do."

> "If I spend my time talking about what someone needs to be able to do, I won't get my own work done—and that's how I get evaluated."

"They just need to be able to do the job—there's no need to make it complicated."

It's understandable why just "getting it done" can be tempting. Vacancies impose extra work on others. Those demands detract individuals from their primary responsibilities. Stretched over a period of time, the quality of every effort is eroded. So . . . let's just do it! Let's bring someone on board—and the faster the better.

That approach simply doesn't work! It may be necessary to do things faster, but the fast way is rarely better. Consider the following four realities.

Reality one

Even freshly minted position descriptions tend to be outdated. The longer those descriptions age, the greater likelihood a stench of irrelevance will develop. The marketplace is in constant turmoil. What an organization needs to be successful today is different from what it required yesterday. Objectives that need to be met keep changing. Skills or aptitudes necessary to be successful continue to shift. Outdated position descriptions aren't helpful—especially when the most accurate statement on them is the tag line declaring the individual accountable for "all other related activities—as assigned."

Reality two

However new, old, or relevant, position descriptions tend to focus on the requisite technical or functional skills required to do the job. That's at least a starting point. Starting points are important—but they're not enough!

If people are to make a positive contribution to their new organization, in addition to technical capabilities, they must also have the aptitudes required to "fit" within a position's unique setting and demands. To not identify with great care what it will take to fit, inevitably plants the seeds for a repetitious search process that squanders time, effort, and money.

Reality three

Hastily considered position descriptions that have been rushed to recruiters provide little helpful guidance. Generalities are not enough to construct an appropriate screening template. They provide no ability to distinguish among the abundance of candidates who have held similarly titled—but vastly different—positions. They force recruiters into making educated guesses and hoping they are correct. With the best of intentions, such guesses frequently harvest more chaff than substance. They waste time and effort, and extend—rather than shorten—the selection process.

Reality four

Executives in the searching mode are also in the selection process. They need, as well as want, a clear description of potential opportunities. They want to land a new position. They also want to contribute to the success of their new organization. To do that, they must fit. Far too often—because of the rush to search that has preceded them—fit factors have been ignored. That leaves candidates attempting to be responsive within an unfocused setting.

One executive in transition voiced a common concern when she said,

"I'm under the impression that a serious disconnect often exists between a recruiter's understanding of the required qualifications and what the client really needs. If no one is clear, what chance is there for success?"

▲▼▲▼

Today's marketplace demand—coupled with its presumed scarcity of candidates—heightens the urgency of the search. Wise stewardship of your corporate assets places a high premium on the need to know which needle you're looking for before you start diving into haystacks.

Speed may be of the essence, but too much hurry can cause a wreck!

CHAPTER

5

Stumbling Forward

It's obvious that today's marketplace keeps changing. Downsizing and rightsizing continue. Mergers and acquisitions abound, as do entrepreneurial ventures. Security-minded executives adopt a low profile in hopes of surviving riff after riff until they can retire with what they expect will be a decent package. Others get caught in the maelstrom of change and are bounced around until they're confronted with new opportunities—mostly with smaller, more transactional, faster-paced, and higher-risk ventures often promising an equity position.

Some executives and professionals are intimidated by what's available. They try, instead, to spread themselves among a combination of part-time positions. Some join 50 percent of the executive workforce who, at one time or another, have made a decision to try their hand at consulting. Some drift into retirement ahead of schedule.

Others thrill to the excitement of a new opportunity. They put in long hours, scramble for a sense of balance—or decide they don't need one—and prepare themselves for the inevitable letdown followed by yet another transition.

Vacancies exist. Whether previously filled or newly created, they provide wonderful opportunities to examine current challenges to a position created by a marketplace in flux. They also make it possible for positions to be redefined and leveraged into greater effectiveness.

Impact of challenge

Unfortunately, as organizations stumble forward toward their future, they frequently miss opportunities. They often fill vacancies, giving little or no consideration to the full spectrum of diversified skills and aptitudes required.

With newly created positions, there's sometimes a need to identify a title and a description broad enough to apply. The goal is to place someone within the appropriate pay parameters of an existing system. Usually that's so diffuse that it's not helpful.

> "This title is not a really good fit," explained one human resource professional. "But the description of activities is vague enough that we can make do. Besides, it's the only thing we have that comes close. If we don't use this one, we're going to have to create a new title, describe a bunch of activities, weight them, and assign points before we can move forward—and I just don't think we have the time."

Because they are in a constantly evolving mode, spin-offs and start-ups can also create complications that further exacerbate an executive's ability to contribute to an organization's success. That's especially true when little attention is paid to focusing the position description. At times, it's admittedly difficult to avoid.

> "I should have learned the first time," said one marketing professional. "I went with a spin-off that had been given a broad mission—so broad we all recognized the need to bring it into greater focus. Most of those who were involved thought I had the experience and expertise needed—and so did I. Our marketplace changed . . . our mission got more narrowly focused . . . and I quickly realized I

wasn't the right person. It was understandable, but it didn't help my career.

"I've just been through that process for the second time. The only difference is that, this time, they've decided to sell the company. My fate is the same. I'm back into search."

Another executive described his perspective in this way:

"I was hired by a fast-growing entrepreneurial group to be its CFO. My initial responsibilities were pretty well described . . . but as we've continued to grow, those responsibilities have changed. A lot more has been added. I've brought in a second staff person, but we can't keep up with everything. We really need a third staff member—but we're not going to be the ones to fill that position.

"We've been told that both of us are being terminated by month's end. The company says it's going to find one or two people who can do what's needed. They just don't understand our workload nor do they recognize that, when we leave, they'll be left with accurate records but no one who knows the history. I wish them well, but I can see they're creating a real mess for themselves. They still haven't taken time to figure out what they really need but that's not stopping them from going out to search. They'll be playing catch-up for a long time."

Even in more traditional settings, the rush to search causes organizations to stumble forward. When a vacancy occurs, it takes time to fill the void. Obvious opportunities will be missed and the pressure to "just get somebody who can do the job" will mount.

Temptations and surprises

People have difficulty resisting these temptations. They're attracted to quick fixes. Consequently, there's often an attempt to shake off any dust accumulated on a current position description. Following a quick scan and some minor tweaking, it's rushed into the search process. People rarely notice how out of touch with reality the description actually is.

"What a surprise!" she commented. "When I interviewed to be the chief financial officer of this organization, the conversation gave me some very definite impressions about what needed to be done.

"Now that I'm here, it seems that the job I'm expected to do isn't the same as the one they said they were hiring me for. There's so much they never told me."

When an executive enters a new position, she or he will always be met by at least some surprises. Sometimes that's due to unintentional oversights. Sometimes what may seem minor to those doing the interviewing may actually have major, but unrecognized, implications. Sometimes the *real truth* is withheld in hopes that it won't dissuade a potential candidate from accepting an offer.

"If we let our candidate for vice president of marketing know how difficult our vice president of sales is to work with, we're likely to wait a long time before we get the position filled," said one CEO.

▲▼▲▼

As you seek to recruit candidates who fit, you will always do some stumbling. Resources will be squandered. The challenge is to minimize that stumbling. Begin by recognizing that your search objective should not be an attempt to have everyone be the same. It's to identify the entire spectrum of interpersonal and team skills required to maximize your organizational potential.

Looking carefully before you step can help you move forward without stumbling!

CHAPTER 6

Confusion Reigns

Words, words, words—liberally used, but what do they mean? To what extent do they point toward a common message? Is everyone always entitled to use her or his own perspective? How viable is personal interpretation, particularly when there's a need for agreement? How useful are different lenses to bring a target into focus?

Clear, concise position descriptions need to be attentive to—and inclusive of—the diverse spectrum of skills and aptitudes required to contribute to your organization's progress. They can be extremely helpful in candidate selection. Most descriptions, however, lack focus.

"I need a vice president of marketing," he said. That statement is an example of a functionally designated position title that begins to limit the search. How sufficient is it? It screens out all those who have not specialized in marketing—but greater clarity is still needed. Or do all those in marketing possess the same abilities and experience? What is the difference between marketing through traditional channels of distribution and e-commerce? Do both venues require the same aptitudes? How important is it to obtain a much more refined focus on the objective of your search?

Missing the focus

There's often a tendency to concentrate on technical and functional aspects of the position. The wording used can employ generalities that confuse the would-be target. As a result, everyone involved in selection has a sense of their individual objective even if others involved in the same effort may—with the best of intentions—be looking for someone quite different. It's understandable how that happens. Consider this excerpt from a position description.

"This individual will be responsible for due diligence, financial analysis, assessment, and, in some cases, negotiation of fiscal transactions with businesses the company is considering for acquisition or joint ventures."

On the surface, the description sounds fairly clear. It's tempting to conclude that this position description adequately describes what's needed—but look more closely.

- What's the focus of the due diligence that's mentioned?

- What actually needs to be accomplished?

- What kind of financial analysis is to be completed?

- What's meant by "negotiation of fiscal transactions with businesses the company is considering for acquisition or joint ventures"?

- What specific skills must one possess to implement the above?

- Who is to determine those skills?

- Is it up to everyone involved in the interviewing process to reach her or his own conclusion regarding what's really needed?

- Is that personal bias to be used to assess the candidate's capabilities?

Another position description states:

> "The successful candidate will be responsible for leading the client's sales and marketing function. The candidate will be expected to create, develop, and execute new and innovative sales and marketing strategies while simultaneously restructuring, directing, and building a combined sales force. The candidate will be responsible for developing new account relationships while maintaining and enhancing current ones."

Once again, a list of activities is provided. These activities suggest it's a highly demanding position. But for exactly what are the interviewers looking? What specific skills will it take to conduct the activities described—and to what degree? From a review of the above description, how can one deduce those capabilities that are necessities?

A third position description states:

"The successful candidate will be responsible for creating and implementing the company's marketing strategies and for developing new client relationships. He/she must possess a thorough understanding of products and capabilities and be able to apply them creatively to customers' needs. The successful candidate must interface with sales departments, production departments, and clients effectively as well as navigate among multiple levels and functions within a prospective company."

Position descriptions frequently sound alike. The greatest similarity is the tendency to generalize functional *activities* to be completed. The determination of what skills are really needed to accomplish those activities within a given organization is then left to each individual interviewer—recruiter, human resource representative, potential peer, and the ultimate decision maker—who may or may not have reached the same conclusion as others.

Experience as criterion

"They said they wanted at least four years of experience," said a recruiter in total frustration. "It was a difficult assignment to locate the combined skill set requested. I dug hard and got almost everything they said they wanted.

"I found a brilliant, socially skillful, highly creative individual who saw himself as a partner. He had great credentials and outstanding references. What I wasn't able to meet was their insistence on those four years of experience. I missed it by a little more than a year. They wouldn't even give this candidate the opportunity to interview."

When they go to search, most companies demand a certain amount of experience—often industry-specific. Unless this criterion is met or exceeded, an otherwise excellent candidate may never be considered.

In days of consistency, when the marketplace was far more tranquil, that experience requirement might have made sense—although the difference between three years and five years of experience can admittedly be minimal. Who is better prepared—an individual who has three years of experience, or one who has a single year of experience repeated five times?

▲▼▲▼

Today, it's important to rethink the role of experience. Business models are constantly being reinvented. New titles for those on the cutting edge spring forth daily—and so do the assumptions of those seeking to fill these positions.

The age in which we live is new. It's one in which everyone has limited experience. Everyone needs to get more and in the same way experience has always been obtained—by doing it. That means taking risks. It means learning by trial and error. It means failing and trying again.

When everyone is looking through a different lens, the likelihood of confusion increases. That makes it very difficult to select an appropriate candidate!

PART II

Growing
Awareness

Functional Skills Aren't Enough

Knowing what specific functional skills are required constructs a *partial* template for screening a candidate's ability to contribute to your organization. To assume that technical knowledge is everything that's needed, however, is a disservice to everyone. There's a much bigger picture to be considered.

Screened and selected against an incomplete template, candidates may be able to function in a timely fashion—*and still fail!* They probably won't fail because of not knowing the technical aspects of their jobs. They're more apt to fail because they don't understand the subtleties of what it takes to work successfully in your particular environment. They'll fail because they either lack or don't use the full range of interpersonal and team skills critical to being productive in your company. They'll fail because they don't fit!

That kind of failure happens far too frequently. It occurs because what it takes to fit is often overlooked in developing position descriptions. It occurs because those conducting the interviews have learned how to work within the nuances of your organization and have forgotten how difficult it was to learn by experience. It occurs because they act on several unrecognized assumptions.

Even though they are often ignored until the unexpected reality of a mis-fit candidate raises its relevance, fit factors are critical requirements for success.

Question the given

Notice how opaque these descriptions of high-profile positions are:

> "The successful candidate will be enthusiastic, resourceful, and have a penchant for new challenges and action. He/she will be expected to act autonomously on the agreed-upon strategies and be a driver of change."

Based on that description, what skill set would you be recruiting for? What aptitudes are required to be "enthusiastic" or "resourceful"? How would you interpret what you heard? To what extent might others reach an identical conclusion based on the same information? What chance is there they might not?

"This individual will be a credible, intelligent, self-confident leader. He/she must be entrepreneurial, able to manage multiple tasks simultaneously and successfully, creative, energetic, and enthusiastic.

"This person will possess demonstrated leadership skills and strong communication skills. He/she must be comfortable making presentations to senior management and have the strength of character and conviction to push back when challenged. This individual will be recognized for a high sense of urgency, results orientation, integrity, and a strong commitment to the business."

These well-intended words provide people with an opportunity to develop their own unique picture of what's needed. What does it mean to be "credible" or "self-confident"? What does it mean to "manage tasks simultaneously and successfully with creativity, high energy, and enthusiasm"? Are these aptitudes or attitudes? Who determines whether a candidate has them? Is it just a sense—a matter of intuition? Even with an excellent and well-planned interview, how does one decide that a candidate has "strength of character and conviction when challenged"?

What message are these words attempting to convey? Is one also to look for interpersonal and team skills—for a certain presence—or both? What kind of selection template is operative?

The following snippets are the complete, non-technical requirements listed in selected position descriptions used by search firms. What questions do they raise for you?

"Client is considering the following attributes in the person they will hire: poise, confidence, and presence."

"Candidate must be entrepreneurial with a proactive, hands-on approach to business; must be willing to take guidance and direction in a family-owned environment; must be detail-oriented and have strong communication skills, team player and motivator, and comfortable working in an ethnically diverse orientation."

Initially, both descriptions sound helpful. Greater consideration, however, reveals that each is permeated by both subtle and obvious pitfalls. Individual interpretations of emotion-laden possibilities can create a potential for misunderstanding and failure. Don't just accept the given—question it!

Broader considerations necessary

Selecting an effective candidate will only happen if you choose someone who possesses the technical *and* the interpersonal *and* the team skills needed to work productively within your unique work environment.

Not everyone will. That's why the selection you make is so critical. You've got to totally do away with imprecise and rushed thinking. You need to carefully define the wide spectrum of skills required to meet your organization's needs, and make certain these skills have a reasonable balance.

Tendency to accept the given

Despite the questions that surface from position description generalities, there may still be a tendency to accept the "given" as sufficient information for identifying the best candidate for your organization. Here are a variety of consequences company leaders have paid for not questioning given information:

> "How I wish we had taken more time," said the COO. "We had our description and used it to conduct our interviews. Admittedly, we were in a hurry to get our selection behind us. Unfortunately, each of us looked at the same thing and saw it differently."

> "As we discussed the qualities of the candidates we interviewed, we realized what a mess we had created for ourselves. We were comparing apples and oranges. We just couldn't get on the same page because we had used different standards."

> "We had hurried to get the vacancy filled and discovered that our rushing actually cost us more time and more effort. We had to go through the whole process again."

▲▼▲▼

Whenever there's an internal drive to get the present behind you—whatever it takes—don't forget that although hustling is important, haste can still make waste. Take the time to broaden your focus. Understand the whole picture. Will it cost you?

Yes, and it will undoubtedly frustrate you as well. But its cost will be far less than if you rush into a decision based on a more limited view.

If you're going to complete the picture, you've got to assemble all the pieces!

What's Missing Matters!

"We draw up a list of everyone we want to
Interview the candidate," stated the vice president
of human resources as she described her company's screening and selection process. "We give
everyone a position description and ask each one
to use it as a basis for questions.

"That's all we do. We don't elaborate on what
we're looking for. We don't have an interviewing
strategy. We like to keep it nice and loose. That
way, we may uncover some additional information
that may be helpful.

"Because most of the interviewers will be working
with a particular executive, we leave it up to them

to know what's needed. When all interviews are
done, we get everyone together and make our
decision."

Many organizations have a similar approach to
screening and selection. Often led by someone
from human resources—with a cursory involve-
ment by a few selected others—a position description is hastily reviewed, perhaps tweaked a bit, and
then dispatched to a recruiter who sets out to meet
stated specifications. Unfortunately, what's asked
for is often not what's actually needed—except in
the most general of terms—and what's missing
matters!

Full of assumptions

It's common for position descriptions to be permeated with assumptions. Titles may point toward the
direction of what's needed—but they are very generalized. They may conjure up impressions, but
they're far from precise. However similar they might
be, what one organization needs in a position may
be dramatically different from what another needs.

Descriptions list activities to be conducted—but
activities may be quite different from the aptitudes
required to obtain results. It's not uncommon to ignore specific interpersonal or team skills a candidate must have if he or she is to contribute to the

success of your organization. The potential for adverse consequences thickens when it's assumed that an executive who has been a star in one organization will automatically glitter in yours. That's not necessarily true.

Need for precision

Organizations are different. One executive may fit well in one organization and fail in another. Unless you take the initiative to clearly identify what specific, rather than general, aptitudes and attitudes are required to work productively within your organization, you can easily hire a candidate who just doesn't fit.

> "I really don't think my clients know what they want," said one recruiter. "They've given me a general description of what they're looking for and I've tried to get them to be more precise—but to no avail. When I push them for more details, they resist—and I don't want to have them pull their search.
>
> "If they want someone from a specific industry, that's what I'll find for them. If they want someone with a minimum of four year's experience, I'll think long and hard before I refer someone who has only three—even if that person's capabilities far exceed

those of my other candidates. Often, I just don't have enough information. I'll take the safe way and get someone who fills the very general description my client provided. At least if I hit most of the markers, they can't fault me if the candidate fails."

It may be understandable for recruiters to limit their searches to the parameters provided—and it's certainly safer although their results may "underwhelm" you. It's hard to heap fault on someone who presents candidates matching your request.

As a corporate leader, however, it's not your job to languish in generalities. It's up to you to screen out all but the most appropriate candidate for your organization. It's up to you to make certain the one you select will possess the requisite abilities and be positioned for success.

Ask and you'll get closer

Every position has multiple customers—the one to whom it reports, peers, direct reports, and representatives of other segments of the business. It may also directly interface with individuals external to your organization. Each of those customers has specific needs that differ from those of others. Implicit in those needs may be the requirement for a diversity of aptitudes and attitudes.

If you are to develop a position description reflective of those needs, you've got to be aware of them. Begin by asking these questions:

- Who are the different customers served by the position?

- What specific products or services is the position holder expected to deliver to them?

Additional questions that sharply focus the desired end result of your search can help you get even closer to your objective.

Ask about the big-picture. Then move toward those that are more specific:

- What is our corporate mission?

- In what way is our mission statement used as a lens through which to view operational and strategic opportunities—including position vacancies?

- To what extent is the description of our vacant position an *accurate* representation of what we really need to implement our mission?

- What assumptions are we making about the spectrum of skills required to successfully fill the vacancy?

- How precise have we been in describing the *specific* functional/technical, interpersonal, and team skills (they're different) required to implement our mission?

Slowing the search and selection process so its generalities can be brought into a more specific focus through intentional questioning is not apt to be popular. It will undoubtedly be met with resistance. Complaints that "our usual routine has worked, so why waste time to change it" can be an expression of amnesia. It's easy to forget how much it has cost each time you've selected a candidate who wasn't right for you. You can be tempted into taking shortcuts that cause you to miss identifying critical information. What's missing truly matters!

▲▼▲▼

When critical information is missing:

- you're forced to act on vague generalities.

- vague generalities send you off on tangents.

- you'll go off on tangents and wind up hiring a candidate—but rarely the best one for your organization's needs.

- you'll fail to select the best candidate for your organization, and it's still going to cost you in time, effort, good intentions, and dollars.

- you'll have to make the same investment again.

If you're going to hit a target, you must first get that target in focus!

CHAPTER

9

Get The Right Fit!

I watched my two-and-a-half-year-old granddaughter, intent in her own world, assemble one of her jigsaw puzzles. Big pieces fit into little hands that had manipulated all but one piece into place.

One piece remained in her hand. Nothing distracted her as she tried to fit it one way and then another. She laid it on top of the vacant spot and patted it with her hands. She tried to press it into place. No matter how she tried, it just didn't fit.

It was, mind you, a perfectly good piece. The only problem was that it was a piece from her older sister's puzzle. Into that other puzzle it would easily slide but—no matter how she twisted and turned and tried to force it—the misplaced piece just didn't fit her puzzle.

Select for fit

The search for an appropriate candidate to fill a vacancy is often like that. You can pick someone who initially looks as though she or he will fit just fine. Some of her or his skills may have the shape and texture of what's needed. Closer examination, however, may lead you to discover that the candidate who appears wonderful may not be the right one for you. Ability to work well with others in a specific context may be proven, but it doesn't necessarily mean a person has what it takes to make a productive contribution in yours. A star one place won't necessarily be a star everywhere.

"I really thought I had made a wise choice," said a vice president of quality about a promotion he had given. "Mike had made a significant contribution in our Northeast operation and, when there was an opening in our California office, I offered him a promotion and a significant bump in salary. I felt good about being able to reward him, and I knew he could do the job.

"He accepted, sold the home they had lived in for several years, uprooted his family, and moved west. It was not an easy move. His junior high school-age children were pulled away from their friends and had to make new ones—not easy at this stage of life. His wife, who had never lived in any other part of the country, had to leave her extended family behind.

"Within a few weeks it became obvious he wasn't working out. He had all the technical skills. He acted with great intentions. He was committed to the company's success and to his own—but he just didn't fit.

"Realizing this was really difficult for his family and for him—and it was also very tough for me. I blew it. I didn't consider everything I should have. Despite my best intentions, I still set him up to fail. I regret that decision more than any other I've made in my career."

Not all pieces fit equally well in a puzzle. Some don't fit at all. However technically capable, not every executive is prepared or able to fill a key vacancy in your organization. She or he may not be able to work productively within its nuances—and that's the fault of no one. It's simply a reality that needs to be recognized. There's no such thing as a universal fit. You've got to get the right fit—and a forced one won't do.

Critical fit factors

In assessing what aptitudes and attitudes an executive needs if she or he is going to successfully fit into your organization, consider these critical factors:

Alignment

Positions exist to meet objectives. If your organization is to implement its mission, what are the objectives it needs? When must they be met? What capabilities must the executive you select possess if she or he is to produce the desired results within established time frames?

Culture

Every organization has its unique characteristics and idiosyncrasies, shaped by its past and the cast of characters who work for it. How have you defined yours? What will it take to be successful within your organization? What questions do you need to ask candidates to get the right information you must have to make your decision?

Expectations

A successful candidate will encounter a diversity of expectations. Although perhaps not expressed, many have been used as the basis for selection. What expectations do you have of the one you will select? How different from yours are the expectations of others? What skills must they have if they are to meet those expectations? How intentional are you in addressing these differences before you begin your interviewing process?

Change

Today's marketplace continues to make new demands on the organization. Changes have already been introduced within your organization. What resistance has resulted from those changes? What additional changes are yet to be introduced? What skills must your new executive have to implement those changes?

With the best of intentions, these fit factors—critical to the choice of a candidate who will be successful—can be overlooked. Without this information, the probability of picking a candidate who will fail will be greatly increased. Get your selection process right—focus on fit!

▲▼▲▼

Selection based on subjectivity is not helpful. Neither is a process permeated with unexpressed assumptions. The success of your organization requires an investment in carefully defining specific functional, interpersonal, and team aptitudes that are critical as a template for selection. Only then are you prepared to hire for fit—and for success.

If you don't hire for fit,

you'll hire for failure!

The First
Fit Factor:
Alignment

It had been a long time since many of the families had seen each other. Work had taken several of us to different parts of the country—but on this leisurely summer day we were all together, as family. Children of all ages from preschool to post-retirement had gathered to remember and to "be."

The grills were hot and salads in place. We said our thanks, ate, and eased into an enjoyment of the day. There were no plans. Some of us older ones reminisced and laughed as we shared stories of growing up together. From the distance of many years, the challenges we remembered didn't seem nearly as daunting as they once did.

Meanwhile, younger ones drifted into clusters—mostly by age—and began getting to know each other as cousins who only periodically spend time together. They had common roots but few moments of shared history. At first it was awkward. How does one get to know all the others? What must one do to fit in with them? What, if anything, can we do together?

The impact of purpose

Then it happened! Someone suggested they build, not an "obstacle course," but a "challenge course." That captured the attention of all the young ones. They agreed on what they wanted to do. They parceled out what needed to be done—down to and including assignments to even the littlest ones. Everyone had to help if this was going to work.

How industrious they were—planning and building. It took nearly an hour before they could try it. Big ones, with little ones in tow, walked through it first so that everyone understood how the course was to be run. Then they ran through it, and invited everyone else to join in their fun.

Earlier in the day, they had been awkwardly active—but when they finally got the idea to build their "challenge course" they became purposeful. A common vision focused their efforts. One helped another. They worked hard, enjoyed the activity, and met their objective.

One could only wish that the executives selected to fill vacancies would be as focused and motivated. They probably won't be! They may be well intentioned and acutely aware of those activities listed in their position description—but unless you have been very clear about what you want them to accomplish through those actions, they're more apt to flounder than achieve. There is, after all, a great difference between motion and progress—between activity and accomplishment.

"I've got this great list of what they want me to be doing," she said, "but I'm having a tough time trying to figure out what the impact of all this activity is supposed to be. I can't seem to get it in context. I'm doing what they asked me to do but it isn't making a lot of sense. I feel like I'm working in a vacuum."

"Take a look at this job description for a vice president of product management I've been offered," he said. "Look at the list of what I'm supposed to be doing—but to what end? I know it's a start-up. I understand they're trying to sort things through. Everything is in a state of flux as they move forward, but that's not helpful for me. If I accept their offer, I want to hit the ground running. But I can't do that if I'm not sure how my job is supposed to contribute to overall corporate success.

"Some folks may be happy to just have the offer. It probably wouldn't bother them. They'd take it, get busy, and try to sort things out along the way. That's not how I work. At different times in my career, I've done most of the parts of this new position but I've never had them all together—and there are a few responsibilities I've never had. I want to be certain that if I accept I can do the job. I really need to know what I'm supposed to accomplish."

That's the purpose of a mission statement. It's to help the people in your organization:

- develop a common vision,

- get themselves beyond "fuzzy" and into focus,

- become purposeful about what must get accomplished if corporate objectives are to be met,

- know what they must personally contribute.

In addition, it provides a rudder people can use to guide the process as they confront strategic and operational threats and opportunities.

Purpose and potential

That's the purpose and it's also the potential of mission statements. Unfortunately, they're often untapped! Dollars, time, experience, and expertise have gone into their development. Introduced with ruffles and flourishes, they often give way to the next management initiative. It leaves behind a jaded workforce that once again feels manipulated by what it considers to have been much ado about little. Here and there, vestiges of direction may remain but are of little obvious relevance.

> "Our mission statement is on display everywhere," said one executive. "It's like wallpaper. It's there, but no one seems to pay much attention to it."

If you're going to hire for fit rather than for failure, there are several critical factors to bring into focus. Vacancies provide you with the opportunity to:

- revisit your mission statement,

- question its relevance amid today's changing marketplace,

- clarify corporate objectives,

- specify what the executive chosen to fill your vacancy must accomplish within what time frame,

- determine skills that are prerequisites to the task.

Alignment—the first fit factor

The first factor to be considered for fit is one of *alignment.* You will be well served if, before rushing to search, you invest your effort in answering questions such as:

- What changes are taking place in our marketplace?

- To what extent are these changes impacting our ability to carry out our stated mission?

- To what extent should our mission be redefined or modified?

- What actions are critical if we are to achieve our mission?

- What objectives must our chosen executive meet if she or he is to contribute to the implementation of our mission?

- What time frame have we set for accomplishing those objectives?

- To what extent does our position description list activities to be performed *or* accomplishments to be achieved?

- What commitments are needed from others in our organization to support the accomplishment of those objectives?

- What skills—technical, interpersonal, and team—must our new executive possess if she or he is to be successful?

▲▼▲▼

Vacancies provide opportunities that can be leveraged. In the name of "busyness"—and because they don't automatically interject themselves—many of those opportunities are missed. To align a position so that whoever fills it can contribute to your corporate success requires an investment of time and thought to describe what they must accomplish. That's the first factor of fit.

Accomplishment is always the result of activities— but activities don't always result in accomplishment!

The Second Fit Factor: Culture

The previous evening's thunderstorm had raised the river's water level and prodded it into higher gear. We only had to guide our canoes for the first couple of miles. Approaching a bend, however, we heard the emerging roar of whitewater. A sudden dogleg left and *it* was in control! Undercurrents and submerged boulders wreaked their havoc, spewing contents in every direction. I was thrown out of "security" and into turbulence—barely managing to catch sight of my canoe as it broke free and careened past my head. I felt scared.

It's possible that the executives you choose to fill vacancies in your organization may have a similar—although unintended—experience. Initially, they may glide through the waters of entry until they are unexpectedly tossed by undercurrents, crosscurrents, and hidden obstacles that both comprise the maelstrom of culture and threaten their ability to survive. That's just as true of countries as it is of companies, and sometimes, in our international marketplace, the two coalesce.

"There's no way I could do my sister's job," she commented as we shared a cup of coffee. "She's the highest-profile woman in her company. Worked her way up. Travels all over the world and keeps running into some strange situations. Just when she thinks everything is flowing smoothly, something happens to upset her assumptions and send her spinning while she tries to make sense of what's happening.

"It's taken her a while to get used to the different ways business is conducted throughout the world. In some countries, men won't negotiate directly with her even though she's the highest-ranking person present from her company. It has to be man-to-man communication so she must take a male assistant with her. She has the authority but, still, they'll only speak to her through a man she's brought along—even when she's in the room.

"On the surface, most things may seem similar but she's become really aware how different cultures can be. If she's not sensitive to the nuances, she can think she's succeeding while she's really only being politely tolerated.

"I don't know how she puts up with it. I couldn't. There's no way I could make it in her world."

It was a chance conversation pointing out that failure to fit the culture can have significant implications. Functional skills and smarts are not enough. If the executive you select to fill a vacancy is to be successful within your environment, he or she will have to have more. The right person must also be appropriately responsive to those threads from which the fabric of your organization's culture has been woven.

Shaped by influences from the past—taken for granted by those who, by trial and error, have learned to navigate it—your culture has its own politics, priorities, and structure that make it different from every other. It will be alien to anyone you select. That's why your selection process must carefully screen for fit.

Culture is politics

> "I just want to do my job," she said. "I have no desire to get caught up in the politics happening in this place."

> "This organization is just too political," he complained. "I just want out."

Politics is an inevitable part of every organization's culture. Overtly or covertly, there will be those more devoted to self-promotion than they are to being productive for the good of the business. There will be those who attempt to control information so they can control others. Some individuals will wield more power and influence than their position title—taken to the broadest of understandings—would suggest.

> "She's his administrative assistant and an institution around here—knows everything about everyone—and she can really be explosive. No one wants to deal with her. That gives her a lot of slack. She pretty much does what she wants and no one calls her to task."

Culture is values

Articulated or not, the past has engrained certain values that guide the way your organization carries out its business. Through activities, those priorities are consistently being reinforced. What does your organization really reward? Is it longevity or personal or team productivity? Does a willingness to run reasonable risks or a way that's more certain receive greater recognition? Is notoriety based on negative or positive comments?

Mixed messages—delivered by actions observed or reported through your organization's grapevine—can be confusing and inhibiting to any executive who wants to contribute to the success of your business.

"They tell us that, to be competitive, we've all got to take risks. We're expected to take reasonable risks," he complained. "That's all right—but why do they hold us up as an example whenever a risk we've taken doesn't achieve everything we hoped it would? I've learned my lesson. From now on, no more risks. I'll just play it safe."

"She said that we were to put the customer first," commented another manager. "I resolved a simple complaint—and then was called on the carpet because I didn't get prior approval of my actions. She can't have it both ways. I can't respond quickly to my customers while waiting for her to give me approval."

Culture is structure

Reporting relationships and the process by which decisions are made reflect another facet of your organization's culture. Some organizations are informal. Some strictly adhere to a chain of command. Some are hierarchical; some use a matrix approach. Some have broad spans of control, others narrow. Some have clearly defined limitations; others—especially because they are in the early stages of development—are vague. Some make decisions authoritatively, others collaboratively.

Because they've been subliminally shaped by the process and haven't taken time to consider these factors, many really aren't certain how they work. There's likely to be as many perspectives as the individuals whom you query.

"I take a collaborative approach to making decisions," responded the CEO. "I run my ideas past my top team, solicit their input, and then we reach a decision."

When asked, the CEO's team members described decision making with him quite differently.

"He comes into the room, tells us the issues, and lays out what he thinks we ought to do about it. Then he asks for our opinions. We don't want to stick our necks out if we see something he's missed so we just go along. It may not be best for the business, but so far it's been best for us."

The culture of your organization includes its politics, its values, and its structure. It's neither right nor wrong. It may be helpful or not very helpful. It is all those overt and covert ways its work environment contributes to or detracts from the effectiveness of the effort your people expend. By trial and error, those who have worked within it have learned to navigate its currents and submerged obstacles even though they may not be able to describe them.

Unless someone takes the time to identify skills required to conquer the turbulence of your organization's culture prior to beginning your search, there's a strong possibility you will select an executive who will not be able to navigate the entrance passageway. With the best of intentions, the candidate will capsize because you haven't selected for fit.

Culture—the second fit factor

Before rushing to search, you will serve yourself well if you invest your efforts in answering these questions that will help clarify your culture.

- What behaviors do our leaders champion by deed as well as word?

- How responsive are we to our customers?

- What gets in the way of our workflow?

- How do we address bottlenecks?

- What personal contributions are given public recognition?

- To what extent is the recognition we give positive or negative?

- What's the relationship between our reward system and the productivity of individuals or teams?

- How do we describe productivity?

- To what extent is our definition "qualitative" as well as "quantitative"?

- How do we celebrate our achievements?

- What is our commitment to being "best of class"?

- To what extent do we invest in the development of each of our employees so they can assist us in being competitive?

- Who will be responsible for describing the environment into which our new executives will be entering?

- What skills—functional, interpersonal, and team—must our new executive possess if she or he is to work within our culture and contribute to our corporate success?

▲▼▲▼

Most executives are instinctively aware that they cannot be equally effective in every culture. At times, however, desperation may tempt them to be delusional. It's up to you to select a candidate who will be able to successfully navigate the turbulence of entry and adapt to your culture.

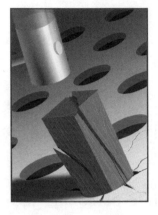

Successful navigation
through the turbulence of
entry depends on knowing
where the currents and
rocks are!

CHAPTER

12

The Third Fit Factor: Expectations

"We're a start-up company," commented the CEO, "pre-IPO. We've had to get some key positions filled while we've been scrambling to figure out what talents we need and how to structure ourselves. Nothing is very clear.

"He looked good on paper—had the kind of experience we wanted—at least that's what we assumed. He also talked as if he had some of the contacts we needed.

"I'm not sure what I expected—but he's been here three months and that's long enough to know he's not meeting my expectations—whatever they are."

Too often an "I'll know it when I see it" approach to expectations is operative. This inevitably leads to selection confusion and to the likelihood that whomever your organization ultimately chooses is apt to fail.

Expectations will differ!

Expressed or not, when you bring new executives into your organization, you have expectations of them—and so does everyone else. Depending on how others relate to the position being filled, each will have a different perspective on what is needed from the new executive to meet perceived objectives. Those needs will help fashion expectations. Prior experience will also contribute to the shaping of expectations. Some will hope that a positive relationship they've had with a predecessor will continue with the new organization. Others who have been less fortunate will hope to avoid a repeat performance.

"I think what we dreaded the most was more of the same. Her predecessor got too involved in the day to day. Couldn't keep her hands off any of the details. We'd get a call at seven in the evening from her—asking for information—and she'd always say it couldn't wait until morning. We'd have to go in at night just to get her what she wanted.

"It's a relief to realize this time we've got someone who gives us clear direction, sets time tables, and then holds us accountable."

Most expectations will be unclear

Generalized expectations will inevitably create a setup for failure. They're too vague to be of much help in focusing the activities of your new executive. Consider this sampling:

"We want you to be a team player."

"We need you to take the lead."

"We need an HR strategy."

"We've got some major communication issues to be resolved."

You've heard similar statements and may even have used some of them. Everyone has expectations to be met—but who will determine when, or if, they are being met? How will their accomplishments be measured? To what degree will my standard and yours be the same? How possible is it that our responses may resonate with dissonance? How will those differences be resolved?

Some expectations will be even more unclear because they remain unspoken.

"Why should I spend time going into that?"

"You know what I need so why should I have to spell it out in detail?"

"I assume you know what you're doing—don't you? Besides, I just don't have the time. I've got more important things to do."

Whenever you act as if everyone shares your worldview, you act against yourself and your organization's success potential. Everyone has her or his own perspective shaped by the lens of personal experience and expertise. Through those filters, expectations are interpreted.

If you want clarity that leads to success, don't assume that:

- because you've said something, it's been heard,

- because someone has heard what you've said, they've understood it the way you intended,

- because someone has understood what you intended, a commitment necessarily follows to respond as you desire.

Priority of expectations will probably not be set

Everyone tends to act on the hope that her or his expectations will receive priority consideration, but there's no way to give priority to everything. Equal priorities means there are no priorities—only disappointments, frustrations, and failures!

Whether by intention or by reaction, however, priorities *will* be set! The request of a hierarchical official is more likely to be given greater attention than a request from someone at a lower level—and that attention won't necessarily be based on the actual importance of the request. Helpful or not, rank has its privileges—even if it obstructs the way to success.

Some priorities will be established by the limitation of time. Because they can't coexist with others, some will be given no priority. When no top priority has been articulated, it will be determined by those who choose to respond according to what they've concluded is important. Either that, or "when they can get around to it." Otherwise, the priority goes unmet.

> "I can't keep up with all the demands," he said. "People think what they want has to take precedence. I understand that but I can't do the impossible. Somebody ought to set some priorities. Until we have common priorities set, they'll have to be satisfied with what I'm doing. Don't blame me if everything isn't done when you want it to be. I'm doing the best I can."

Despite that plea, as soon as one's expectations fail to be given proper priority (according to them)—blame will be placed. Words will be directed and fingers pointed at the one who did not meet expectations in order of self-interpreted importance—not at the ones who failed to establish priorities.

Expectations—the third fit factor

Clearly defined, expectations provide valuable input into search and selection. Skimmed over, they impede the choice of someone who can make a positive contribution. They will also feed this lament of those who fail to fit.

"If I had only known."

"Why didn't you tell me what you wanted?"

"How was I supposed to know?"

Through personal as well as professional experience, you've probably learned that expectations must be known before they have any chance of being met. If they're not, failure will result. No one wants that to happen but it will—unless you have clarified your expectations, prioritized them, identified what aptitudes they require, and have incorporated this data into your search assignment.

These questions help you focus on your expectations:

- What were the strengths of the previous position holder?

- Who will be the customers of the one you select?

- What are the critical success factors of each customer?

- How do you want your new executive to manage others?

- How do you want him or her to resolve differences?

- What role do you want the executive to take in developing his or her people?

- How do you want the new executive to relate to peers?

- What possible difficulties could be encountered working with peers?

- How do you want your new executive to keep you informed?

- How do you want him or her to present bad news?

- What limits is he or she expected to adhere to?

- What commitment to professional development do you expect?

- In what ways do the expectations of others— who are also customers of the position—differ?

- What steps are needed to prioritize the diverse expectations that different customers have of the position?

- What skills—technical, interpersonal, and team—must your new executive possess to meet your expectations?

▲▼▲▼

The archaeology of every expectation reveals multiple assumptions that will influence your screening. These assumptions must be recognized before you can get clarity. Clarity is present when two things happen: the desired outcome has a standard against which it can be measured, and everyone knows that standard.

Expectations can't be met until everyone clearly knows what they are, knows their priority, and knows how they'll be measured!

13

The Fourth Fit Factor: Change

Although it was several years ago, I remember it well. Our organization was adapting to a computer-literate world. Appropriate hardware and software had been installed. At all levels, individuals were involved in generic and position-specific training. We assumed that our most immediate ROI would be the ability to do more with less.

I was the CEO. Prominently displayed on my desk was a computer. It was a clear signal to everyone that we were serious about the change. Intellectually I knew it would positively impact our ability to compete. If we were to be prepared for the immediate and long-term future, there was at least a degree of mastery to be attained.

There sat my computer and on my chair sat I. Except for an occasional stare, there was little contact between us. Confronted by the need to change, I kept resisting.

Change isn't new!

Every healthy system is in a constant state of change as it takes in data (input), transforms or changes it, then produces an output. That's always been true. It will continue to be true.

What's different about change today is the rapidity with which it confronts us. It incessantly demands us to react.

"It's a whole new world," he commented. "I've never been exposed to anything like this.

"We're trying to capitalize on a very limited window of opportunity before we go public. Everything is up for grabs. We're overwhelmed, and we keep wondering what we're missing.

"I feel like I'm on the front end of a rushing locomotive laying track as we go. It's exciting. I just hope we can hang on and make it."

Change is always present. There's no escaping it. Some of it is helpful. Some is irrelevant. Some is forced before its time. Some is delayed long enough so that opportunities are missed. You've probably experienced at least a sampling of all of this. Both dramatically and subtly, your organization has been changing and continues to change.

Change requires new behaviors

Recent decades have witnessed the cascading impact of wave after wave of change. From the glacial speed of industry giants to the instant response of virtual companies, from individuals being used as pairs of hands to being valued as assets—change has persisted. Through downsizing, rightsizing, mergers, acquisitions, spin-offs, and start-ups, change has also left its imprint.

Priorities and values have shifted. Loyalty in both directions has become a rare commodity. The acquisition of new skills—technical, interpersonal, and team—has become critical. Whatever they have been, each change has produced a demand that things be done differently—and there's no letup.

"What we're planning for now isn't going to last very long," she said. "It's but one step in a constant race toward success.

"How are we going to cope with all that's happening? Will we be ready and able to shift direction fast enough? Do we dare to risk what it may take to be successful? Do we have enough capital? Do we have the skills? What more do we need? How will we develop them? What if we risk and we're wrong?

"It's exciting! It's scary! It's a constant roller coaster ride and it's not going to stop. I just hope I can keep myself up to speed."

New behaviors threaten security

Whenever change dislodges us from our comfort zone, it's instinctive to ask, "What does this mean for me?" Individuals may have hunches, but there's little certainty. One is only aware that opportunity and threat coexist, triggering subliminal fears that imagine the worst. Quickly those fears take control, frequently throwing the organization into fibrillation.

"It's one wave after another," he said. "Nothing ever really settles down into a routine. Just when we think it has, the pot gets stirred and we start rippling again.

"Living with all this uncertainty places us under high stress. I don't like working this way—not knowing what's going to happen next—and I really don't know how long I can cope with it."

Security that's threatened produces resistance

In an attempt to rebalance, individuals instinctively resist the imposition of change—often outside their awareness. This attempt at self-preservation can take several different forms. Some are obvious. Others are so subliminal they go unrecognized— even by their perpetrators.

Individuals can fight with one another or they can take flight—choosing either to leave or to keep a low profile until the current storm passes. They can become coercive—putting others down in an attempt to provide themselves with greater prestige. They can collude with others to rid the situation of the one suggesting change. They can become overly dependent on the one who is introducing change, in hopes that closeness will provide protection.

Change—the fourth fit factor

Into this flux, you are now preparing to select and place a candidate who you want to be successful. It's not likely you'll want this person to enter and maintain the status quo. It's more probable you'll want him or her to make an impact, to bring about even more change—and that means more stirring, more stress, and more resistance.

Most of the candidates you'll consider have had change done to them and have imposed it on others—but few will have had the opportunity within their professional careers to learn how to actually be an agent of change. It's important, therefore, to assess the challenges of change within your organization and to clarify, rather than assume, what skills your candidate really needs to command if she or he is to be successful. Before you begin your search, it's helpful to answer the following questions.

- What changes are taking place in our marketplace?

- How are those changes impacting our primary competitors?

- Where do they have a competitive advantage?

- Where are they most vulnerable?

- What's our competitive advantage?

- Where are we most vulnerable?

- What opportunities are current marketplace changes providing for us?

- What must we do to leverage those opportunities?

- What's the downside impact if we don't?

- What's the ripple effect of these changes on each of our position descriptions?

- What changes have we introduced in the past six to twelve months?

- How has resistance to those changes been expressed?

- What additional changes must we make if we are to leverage our opportunity to be competitive?

- What's our strategy for introducing that change?

- How realistic is the timetable we've set?

- How will those changes impact the way we do business?

- What resistance do we anticipate?

- What internal/external resources do we currently have in place to support the implementation of proposed change?

- How do these realities shape what the executive we select needs to accomplish and within what time frames?

- What technical, interpersonal, and team skills must our new executive possess if she or he is to successfully lead our change initiative?

▲▼▲▼

Change is inevitable. You can't escape it. In today's marketplace, it's not enough to be able to manage it. The candidates you select must be capable of effectively leading and leveraging change. If they can't, they won't fit what you need—and if they don't fit, it's extremely difficult for them to succeed.

Skill makes the difference between imposing and successfully introducing change!

PART III

Invitation to Action

CHAPTER

14

Get a Different Perspective

During a presentation I was making to a group of
senior executives, one of them asked, "Whatever
happened to corporate loyalty?"

"People quit being loyal to the company when we
quit being loyal to them," responded another
member of the audience.

Once upon a time, loyalty was mutual. Individuals
had a job, knew what it required, and were glad
they had it. They were and remained company people even after their careers were capped with a
gold watch and they strolled into their sunset years
of retirement.

In the emerging reality created by the swirl of "dot com" start-ups, such security no longer exists. There is less and less certainty. Today's marketplace hurtles from one transition to the next and the cacophony of its challenge demands that everything be constantly rethought. That's a critical necessity for success and it's often resisted.

> "So far I've been pretty successful," one CEO commented. "I've been able to avoid all of this Internet stuff. I don't even use e-mail and I see no need to get started—particularly at this stage of my career."

It's easy to hear those remarks and conclude that however successful he may have been, the curtain is about to come down on his career—and we'd be right. It's important to recognize, however, that he's not alone in his reluctance.

Many of today's seasoned executives have been through a plethora of changes. Some still remember shifts. . . .

From	To
electric typewriters	computers
carbon paper	copiers
hard wired communication . . .	cell phones and beepers
personal secretaries	do it yourself
interoffice memos	e-mail

```
mail . . . . . . . . . . . . . . . . . . . . fax

push marketing . . . . . . . . . . . pull marketing

management by fiat . . . . . . . . management by team
                                    input
```

. . . and many more. They also remember how each of those changes altered the way they had become accustomed to working. They know what it's like to be pushed out of their comfort zone—time after time. Many have had enough of adapting.

As things continue to change, even younger executives are resisting—although perhaps not as overtly. Some resistance may be outside awareness. Some may even be infecting your company's screening and selection process.

You've got to think differently

When vacancies were being filled, companies once looked for:

- technical competence

- consistent work history

- long-term commitment

- unquestioning allegiance

- willingness to take direction

These were the values on which success was built—but things are different now. Many of those attributes are no longer available and, even if they were, they would probably be about as relevant as carbon paper. Once essential, now they're more of a curiosity.

Yesterday's criteria are important if you want to understand the past. It is not the focus that's needed, however, if you want to select for the future success of your company. Just as the marketplace has shifted, so must your perspective. It's critical!

Think differently about retention

After you've gone through the arduous task of identifying, interviewing, selecting, and waiting for your new executive to get up to speed, it would be nice to think that he or she would stay for a while so you could experience a benefit for an extended period of time. Alas, that's probably not going to happen. One recent study suggested that most executives will change positions at least every four years.

Every organization has always been a pass-through organization. The only question was the length of time it would take—and that time is getting shorter.

> "I've got a great deal," said the newly selected
> COO. "I've got options and we're going public in a

couple weeks. Each year for the first five I get another 20 percent vested.

"I don't know how long I'll stay around. With the experience I'm going to get, I may be able to pull out in two or three years and head my own show. I should be able to walk with at least a couple million and be on to my next challenge. That's what I've got to do to take care of me."

These days, incessant change keeps transforming the marketplace for everyone. New skills and attributes necessary to remain competitive are constantly being identified. What you need your executives to contribute today differs from what you needed yesterday—and it's also apt to be different from what you're going to need in the near future.

"I don't know how long I'll need her," said the CEO of a "pre-IPO dot com" organization. "Things are going to change as we push forward and we may or may not need what she has to offer.

"Right now she has information and insight that no one else on my team has—and she has some great contacts that are going to be very helpful. That's why I need her—at least for now—but I have no idea for how long.

"I also know that the cram course she'll go through here will make her just that much more valuable to someone else. In a short time, her opportunities will increase exponentially so I expect I'll lose her."

Changing positions used to be considered a sign of an unreliable employee. Your experience and mine has taught us that's not necessarily true. Today's executive *expects* to change positions as often as eight to ten times throughout her or his career. If you want to search and select for your company's future success, you've got to anticipate that reality.

Think differently about the significance of soft skills

"Not too many years ago," he said, "what I really needed was a broad back, strong arms, and an extra pair of hands.

"It's no longer brawn that's needed—now it's brains. Even though I've been in business for a long time, I have to realize I don't have all the answers. I've got some of them—but things are getting so specialized, everybody tends to have only partial insight.

"But brains aren't enough. They've also got to know how to deal with people if we're going to figure out how to maximize what we each bring."

These words of wisdom and insight were spoken by a long-term senior executive who has a hard-earned awareness that a company's competitive edge is not going to be obtained by directive. The experience-shaped expertise of each executive must be tapped—and can best be done through what we know as "soft skills."

▲▼▲▼

For a long time "soft skills" have been denigrated—but no longer. Technical skills are not sufficient. Giving orders to get results is proving to be less and less effective. We've got to learn to speak *with* each other, not just *at* each other.

We've got to learn how to manage differences, to support each other's professional development, to motivate, to get and maintain commitment, to explore and evaluate alternatives if we are to benefit from each other's insights. We've got to help each other be the best we can be. It's a new workplace. Only those who think differently and have well-honed interpersonal and team skills are equipped to produce success. Not everyone does.

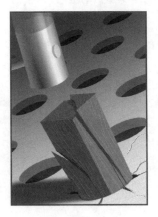

Future opportunities can't be grasped as long as we keep waiting for the past to repeat itself!

CHAPTER

15

The New Criteria

"How are we supposed to cope?" asked the senior human resources executive. "Everything keeps changing. Nothing stays the same.

"I used to think I had many of the answers. Now I'm just overloaded with questions."

"We're trying to hire people who will make a real contribution, but with today's changes we're not even certain what we should be looking for."

Changes signify that every assumption you've been making is under challenge. They also require you to discover what new questions need to be asked so you can effectively proceed toward the future.

As you prepare to hire for today's transitioning reality, it's important that you begin by clarifying the objective of your search.

Are you looking for people who:

- want a job or who see themselves as a resource?

- want to work *for* your organization or *with* it?

- want to be an employee or a business partner?

- want specific direction or are willing to risk taking unprompted initiatives?

It's tempting to gloss over these questions. Don't! They're not as simple as they may seem. Their nuances are critical. Only after you've carefully thought through your responses are you ready to expand your search beyond technical skills. Then you can make a concentrated effort to screen for the aptitudes and attitudes your new executive must possess if she or he is to help leverage the success of your organization.

You should intentionally screen for a candidate who:

- brings a different perspective,

- is willing to push back,

- knows how to raise questions,

- values respect,

- is willing to put her or his own skin in the game,

- understands herself or himself as a resource,

- consistently invests in her or his personal development, maintains balance.

Brings a different perspective

"Birds of a feather often do flock together," even in the corporate world. That's understandable. There's a certain comfort level in being around others who think and act in ways similar to yours. It's also understandable how one who isn't always on the same page would slow things down by asking, "Yes . . . but . . . have you also considered?" This person may appear to be a boulder in the path of progress.

In today's demand for rushed decisions and actions, it's easy to get tempted and yield to quick-fix solutions, forgetting there's always more than one viable way to address any situation. Each of those ways has its unique advantages and disadvantages.

Different perspectives can gift you with wisdom, insight, and subtle nuances, adding significant value to your efforts.

Select an executive who will expand your vision to embrace more options!

Is willing to push back

"If he wants your opinion, he'll tell you what it is," commented one executive, describing the individual to whom he reported.

That old school stereotype suggests there's only one right approach—held by the one who has the power. Today there's a growing recognition of that fallacy. There are many options which, if pursued, can help clarify and expand opportunities.

Those whom you select will not serve you well if they let you push ahead only focused on the alternative you see and advocate. You need their constructive resistance to strengthen your initiatives—but don't assume they'll automatically provide it.

Look for executives whom you can trust to challenge your opinions, and don't betray their trust when they do!

Knows how to raise questions

All conversation consists of comments and questions. It's questions that frequently possess the greater potential for usefulness—unless you react to them as threats.

> "Whenever someone raises a question, I instinctively feel like I'm being interrogated," said one COO. "I immediately go on the defensive. I stop listening and miss all kinds of new possibilities. I know that's not helpful, but it is what I do."

Questions need not be viewed as a challenge to you and your authority. Appropriately raised, they can help you move beyond current assumptions and discover new options that can lead to greater success.

If the ability to raise questions is so critical, why is such a small portion of a screening interview devoted to listening and responding to those raised by the candidate? What is learned when, with but a few moments left, the interviewee is finally given your permission to ask any questions he or she has? Do you hold off because you fear these questions will cause you to lose control? What does this suggest?

An executive who has developed the ability to be appropriately inquisitive can be a valuable asset. Listen for this skill!

Values respect

> "You salute the rank, not necessarily the individual," I was instructed. "It's the position you're honoring, not the person."

Respect, or at least deference, is often given based on position—and it's usually offered to one regarded as a superior. One-way respect is important. Yet success in today's marketplace makes two-way respect even more important.

The greatest respect one can provide to others is the readiness and willingness to listen to the point of *comprehending their intent* as they speak—and responding only then. Frequently that doesn't happen. Most individuals are so impressed with what they have to say that they are poor listeners. Initial words trigger the editing of a response that's probably not going to be on target because it was prematurely crafted. As a result, the positive potential of any collaborative effort will be purloined.

When searching for an executive, screen for one who respects others to the point of valuing what they have to contribute—even if they differ!

Is willing to put her or his own skin in the game

> "I want someone willing to run risks with us," said the CEO gathering individuals who would guide his start-up "I want someone willing to do some sacrificing up-front in favor of a hope for a 'bigger bang for the buck' later on. They've got to put their own skin in the game."

Job security is less certain today than ever before. There's a far greater degree of risk that must be confronted. Along with that risk comes greater opportunities—some of which may bear fruit. Some may die on the vine.

A willingness to share both risk and the potential for reward is critical in today's marketplace. It sharpens the focus one brings to decision making, fosters commitment, and strengthens accountabilities to others for one's actions.

Either you'll succeed, or you'll fail—together. In selecting your new executive, choose someone who is prepared to share both the risks and the rewards with you.

Understands herself or himself as a resource

It's time to quit looking for someone who wants a job.

However well intended, job seekers will not make a significant contribution to the success of your company or organization. Their perspective is too limited. It's too focused on personal security and too rarely integrated with corporate strategy.

Instead, you need individuals who bring a "partner" mind-set to the table. You need people who understand themselves to be in the business of providing a resource for the good of the whole, and who are very clear about the resource they bring. They also need to be acutely aware of their limitations.

No one is capable of being all things in every situation. That's reality. Each person on the team you are building has certain capabilities—technical, interpersonal, and team. Each person also has certain capabilities yet to be developed.

Carefully determine what resources you need to maximize corporate success. Evaluate the resources you have. Identify what additional resources you need. Screen for them—and plan how to leverage them.

Consistently invests in her or his own development

How long will any business be successful if it contents itself with the products and services it is currently capable of providing? What future is there for any individual who chooses to rest on her or his laurels? What's ahead for those who ignore the need for constant personal and professional initiatives to keep their competitive edge?

With the abundance of changes occurring today, there's an almost frenetic demand to provide *relevant* goods and services. Research and development must have the highest priority. Any business rejecting that challenge will drift into irrelevance and render itself incapable of competing. That can also happen with individuals.

If you're deciding to partner with executives who present themselves as a resource, doesn't it make sense to have them describe the initiatives they are presently pursuing to expand their own ability to be competitively positioned?

Maintains balance

"You can't get sand out of an empty bucket."

That's what my Mother used to say—and she was right. Buckets have to hold something before anything can be dispensed from them. Many times we've proven that to ourselves and have concluded, "I'm just out of gas." "Right now I haven't got anything left to give."

Demands placed on our professional life can easily—and subtly—take precedence over all other facets of our lives. However we may attempt to justify our actions, we have personal relationships as well as professional ones. We also have intellectual, creative, and spiritual aspects. Nurturing them and keeping them in balance is critical. Should we fail, we deplete our ability to pursue success. We have nothing left to give.

That's also true for any executive you ask to join your company. Balanced, they have much to contribute. Spent, they may even be frenetically active but unable to significantly contribute to the success of your organization. Search carefully. After all, how helpful is an executive who is living an out-of-balance life?

▲▼▲▼

Today's marketplace has altered the way we need to get things done if we're going to remain competitive. There's little room for isolated performances. There's much need for the collaborative effort of individuals committed to the leveraging of professional and personal skills for the good of the organization. Additional aptitudes as well as a dramatic shift in attitude are critical to success.

If you're screening for executives who can contribute to the competitive edge of your organization, you've got to know what skills they—and you—need!

E Pluribus Unum

"We talk a lot about teamwork," remarked one executive, "but talk is as far as we get. Most of the time, even within our separate functional areas, we tend to think and operate in silos.

"We've got lots of cross-cut issues—issues that impact several of us. Sure, they impact each of us differently, but we really should deal with them. Let's face it. Ignoring them, like we usually do, resolves nothing."

Calling oneself a team while continuing to work in isolation is common—and whenever it occurs, there is an adverse impact on an organization's potential for success.

The search for a new executive often tends to be done with minimum collaboration. For example, one major pharmaceutical company was experiencing frequent breakdowns on its packaging line. In addition to delayed shipping, those breakdowns also impacted the production, quality control, and engineering departments.

To resolve the problem, a packaging engineer position was approved. The engineering department was assigned to develop the job description. With relative ease, a list of skill requirements—almost entirely technical—was presented for review before going to search. It was then suggested that the description also be presented to other involved departments for their comments.

> "Why should we do that?" was the reaction. "We know what a packaging engineer should be able to do. What will QC, Production, and Packaging have to contribute?"

Eventually a meeting was held at which the description was presented. Reaction was immediate! No one questioned the technical skills that had been identified as necessary—but there were many questions about what had *not* been identified. Those questions pertained to skills needed to work in a high-stress environment, to listen to diverse opinions, and to help involved players from different areas of accountability reach resolution even though the packaging engineer had no authority over the participants.

> "You can get somebody who knows how to fix the problem," one of the position description developers commented, "but unless they have some of these other skills, while they're fixing one problem they'll be creating a lot more."

To prepare your screening template so that your organization can hire right, answer these questions as they pertain to the primary tasks and responsibilities of your new executive:

- Who is involved?

- What needs to be accomplished?

- What deliverables do we expect?

- What priority will we establish?

Who is involved?

No position is an island. Each has several customers—other departments, peers, direct reports, external customers and suppliers, and the one the position reports to—to whom it provides services and goods. Each has unique needs and expectations that differ. Whether or not they receive a hearing, they will have their expectations.

If the position is to be defined so that the most appropriate candidate can be identified and selected, it's critical that each customer has input—and surrogates will not, and cannot, be as accurate. That doesn't mean using surrogates won't be attempted. Under the excuse of being too busy, many primary customers will attempt to pass off their responsibility to determine what's needed to their human resource professional.

Those with and for whom your new executive will be working know best what they need. Prodding them to provide that information may well be necessary. Remember, to have less than their reasoned input will create a failure trap for your new executive and your organization. It will also prolong your search and lead to erosion of productivity, missed opportunities, diminished morale, and squandered time and corporate resources.

What needs to be accomplished?

That's inevitably an easier question to ask than to get answered. Despite protests to the contrary, consensus about the specifics of what needs to be accomplished is often lacking. Consequently, much time is wasted discussing proposed solutions—while issues to be resolved remain unclear. With no concurrence, it's possible to be in motion but impossible to make forward progress.

Answered *sequentially*, these questions will bring clarity:

- What are we trying to accomplish?
  (How will we measure our results?)
  (How will we know we're successful?)

- What are our limitations?
  (What resources do we have—time, finances, people, and expertise?)

- How will we work?
  (What options do we have?)
  (How will we coordinate our efforts?)

- Who will do what?
  (Who will be accountable for what?)
  (How will we maintain accountability?)

The results customers collectively expect your newly hired executive to achieve must be defined. If they're not, all the homework needed to identify required skills hasn't been completed. To go to search before this task is accomplished is premature, and will constitute a major contribution to the failure potential of the person selected.

What deliverables do we expect?

Everyone wants her or his expectations to be met. That's understandable but it's not realistic. Depending on what they need to conduct their activities, each primary customer will have specific and different expectations. Some will be mutually exclusive. Some will be unrealistic.

Although "I'll know it when I see it" is not necessarily the best way to select an executive who will effectively contribute to your organization, it's frequently substituted for the more focused effort that was just suggested.

Interviewing numerous candidates and using the information you receive to further alter and tweak the position description is an iterative refinement process. It's one that can be helpful but it's not efficient. If you have the patience and resources to support a "trial and error" interviewing approach to figure out what you really need—hoping you get it right—then the need for clarity can be temporarily bypassed.

From personal as well as professional experience, however, many of us have learned that expectations not stated have very little chance of being met. To avoid this potential for failure, make certain the primary customers of the position for which you are hiring clearly state what they expect.

What priority will we establish?

What's the real reason why such a lack of position definition exists before an organization goes to search? Is it really that we are too busy? Is it that we fail to see linkages between successfully getting the job done and the executives we select? Is it that we really don't know how to go about defining what's needed? Is it that human resource personnel are accessible, ready to help, and can serve as a convenient scapegoat if things should go awry? Or might it be the fantasy belief that our needs will, of course, be met first, thus creating the reluctance to clarify and prioritize expectations as a foundation step in the strategic search for a new executive?

Perhaps it's a combination of all of the above, shaped by additional factors not yet mentioned. Whatever the reason, if you're committed to the initial and long-term success of a new executive, you serve yourself well by identifying and prioritizing expectations.

Since all cannot receive equal treatment, what's the standard you will use to rank-order their importance? Will a superior's request always have top priority? Should it? Is there a time when, for the good of the total organization, another should be given priority? What should determine when the request of one peer should be given priority over another? How should the importance of simultaneous requests of different functional areas be assessed? Is there a time when the need of an external customer should supersede that of an internal customer? What agreed-upon principles are in place to provide wisdom and guidance?

▲▼▲▼

Positions do not exist in a vacuum. They support many others in the successful fulfillment of their initiatives to meet your corporate objectives. Their needs and expectations comprise a mosaic of demands. Those demands are a tangled web, which can trap new executives and cause them to fail. As you prepare to search for a new executive, recognizing this diversity of demands is critical. What you need as a starting point is a customer-responsive position description so that, from the diversity, one common understanding can be created.

If you're going to market
to recruit an executive, be
careful what you look for—
you may get it!

Reality Check

You've brought the primary customers together. You've carefully listened to each other and reached verbal consensus. Now you're ready to go to search.

I'm really quite pleased with all our work," said one primary customer involved in the process, "but it hasn't been easy.

"I never realized how differently we each relied on this position. It's no wonder we've had conflict in the past. I just hope this works.

"I think we've got a real good handle on what skills we would like our new executive to have. If

our recruiter can only follow through and find us
this kind of candidate, we should be golden."

His statement, "what skills we would *like* our new executive to have," raises a critical issue of reality. After all the effort that's been expended, to want what you want is understandable. Everyone is entitled to dream, at least for a moment. After the dream, however, comes the need to wake up to reality.

You have certain wants—certain things you would like to have. Every want, however, is not a necessity! It might be nice to want your new executive to be able to walk on water—and to part it, too—but if all you actually need is someone who can drink water, then your description may be a self-deception influenced by grandiose wishes.

After you've reached customer consensus, getting to the reality of search requires you to continue with these steps:

- Establish the range

- Provide resources

- Demonstrate commitment to success

Establish the range

I recently attended a country fair featuring the

handicraft of many weavers, carvers, potters, tinsmiths, glassblowers, and woodworkers. It was interesting to stand back and observe. Certain impulse buyers simply pointed to what attracted them and whipped out a credit card. Others compared one artisan to another as they meticulously noted how each had plied her or his craft. It was clear that different standards prevailed. Neither was right or wrong—just different. Some were clearly utilitarian in their selection—will it do what I want it to do? Others, concerned with artistry, tended to be more exacting.

As usual, I was among the more picky shoppers. In most things I'm not satisfied with just having something that will do the job. I want the very best—and sometimes that causes me to overlook what I could really use because I keep looking for what I perceive as higher quality.

At times, that puts me out of touch with reality. I don't always need what I want. *Between the best of all possible worlds and what's livable, there's quite a range.* Whether I'm considering a handcrafted object or the qualifications of the next executive to be screened, it's helpful to remember that. It gives me options.

As you prepare to go to search, it can also be helpful to establish the range of what's acceptable to you. Review your customer-responsive position description and establish your options. If you could have your "druthers," what are all the aptitudes and attitudes that you would like your new executive to possess? If you can't get them all—and you won't be able to—which ones can you do without, although perhaps reluctantly? Which must you make absolutely certain that your new executive brings?

Provide resources

An athlete without an arena or game equipment is ill equipped to be in championship contention. She or he must have resources, or winning a championship just won't happen. Your new executive must also be well equipped, if she or he is to succeed.

> "One of the first things I've got to do is to assess the team I inherited," said one recently landed executive. "I've already been told that some of their efforts need to be redirected. Now I'll have to find out if they're able to make the shift.
>
> "If they can't, some weeding will be necessary. But to make it all happen, I've got to buy a little time and make sure I've got enough budget.
>
> "If I don't have the resources I need, I'm not going to make it."

That's true for all executives. If they don't have the

resources they *need*—not want—their potential for success is drastically limited, no matter how intelligent and talented they are.

Dan was selected by a group of turn-around investors—all of them attorneys—to replace a CEO whom they had terminated because the expected numbers weren't being met. After six weeks of initial assessment, he reported that success was possible only if a significant investment was made within a very limited window of opportunity.

> "We haven't budgeted for that contingency," was the response he received. "We'll work it into next year's budget. No problem—but it will be eight months before you can use it."

However talented they may be, if new executives are to succeed, they must have the resources they need—the right people, sufficient time, and an adequate budget. Without those elements, their ability to contribute is nullified.

Demonstrate commitment to success

> "What a difference," she said. "In my last position I had the responsibility for managing million-dollar projects and it was frustrating.

"Every step I wanted to take, every dollar I wanted to spend—even though it was within a budget that already had been approved—I had to get another approval. Not only that, I had to state my case—and win it. I always felt any success would be in spite of them, not because of them.

"What a difference in this new situation," she continued. "I consistently get the feeling this organization wants me to succeed.

"I still run multimillion-dollar projects—larger ones than before—but I have input into my budget and once it's approved I'm free to spend it as needed. There's no more asking for permission. I'm trusted."

Your new executive is not going to be successful alone. He or she needs your demonstrated commitment to success—not just words. *Trust* and *collegiality* are integral to the commitment they need from you.

To hold your executive accountable for results yet insist on micro managing her or his activities is to treat the person not as a professional but as a marionette. Expecting him or her to run everything by you for concurrence before taking action is no way to demonstrate your commitment to the work being done. Either the people you put in charge are given the authority to make decisions within realistic parameters—and held appropriately account-able—or they are not. It's a matter of *trust!* If you trust them, let them take action. If you don't, why keep them around?

▲▼▲▼

You're never going to get everything you want in a new executive. She or he may have several of the attitudes and aptitudes you'll identify as necessary. She or he will have others you may not have iden-tified as important—and she or he will be missing some you wanted.

However capable new executives are, they sim-ply won't know all the answers. At times they will be unaware of certain critical information and per-spectives. They will be able to identify some alter-natives and will be blind to others—unless someone points them out. In so many ways, they will be just like you. That's reality!

Fantasy tempts you to both enjoy and avoid— but success demands you deal with reality!

CHAPTER 18

Your Potential Partner's Perspective

"I hadn't realized how out of touch I had become," said one company president in transition. "I was like a robot. Lately, I've taken time to rediscover what it's like to become somewhat human. It's been fun watching my eight-year-old play softball. I've almost learned how to deal with six or seven walks in a row. That's a real lesson in patience.

"Many nights each week, my wife and I take long strolls through our neighborhood. We hold hands . . . get an ice cream cone . . . share our hopes . . . our fears . . . our dreams. I'm getting to know her all over again.

"It puts a different perspective on things. Pushing to be at the top isn't all that matters. There are some other things that give more meaning."

A considerable degree of meaning can usually be found in professional relationships—but executives are increasingly realizing that, when they look back at what they've accomplished, they'll rarely regret not spending more time working for their company. They may, however, regret not spending more time thinking outside the box, not weighing options before making decisions, and not keeping themselves in balance.

After you've decided what your range of acceptable options is for the executive you are preparing to hire, it's critical to remember that *your* hopes and expectations are not the whole. They're only *your* perspectives. There are also the fears, needs, and wants your potential partner is bringing to the table.

Fears can exist at different levels. As they become more desperate in their search, some executives panic. On the surface, they may appear serene while beneath, with stomachs churning, they're scrambling as fast as they can. In that condition, their truth tends to become malleable. Risk adversity intensifies and their ability to make a positively significant impact is limited. Paralysis motivated by fear sets in and they become their own worst enemy.

More rational fears also exist. When inheriting the mess of a hemorrhaging organization, a project significantly off schedule, or a team in disarray, there's an understandable fear people may be held accountable for a situation not of their own making. In today's spin-off environment, there's also the fear of personal consequences resulting from a merger or acquisition—particularly if it occurs shortly after your new executive has been hired. These concerns not only deserve recognition; they also need to be specifically addressed, *in writing*. It's just part of the flip side involved in establishing a trusting relationship with a partner.

Today's potential partner is also likely to be concerned about her or his ability to:

- Maintain balance

- Remain professionally competitive

- Benefit financially from her or his ability

Maintain balance

"It was a great opportunity," she said. "They offered me a significant bump in salary, plenty of challenge, a budget that was more than adequate. It was really tempting.

"Then, at the last moment, my would-be boss said, 'You need to know there's some travel involved.'

"When I asked how much, he told me that I would be on the road about three-quarters of the time. That ended any consideration on my part.

"I have no obligations that would prevent me from traveling that much, but it just wasn't appealing. Some travel is understandable, but I'm basically a homebody with hobbies I thoroughly enjoy. It's how I keep myself in balance."

Today's executives are frequently torn between allegiances to professional and personal relationships and loyalty to "self." It's the commitment to be a good parent as well as a good professional. It's the need to be accessible as a caregiver for elderly parents. It's the need to stop a treadmill existence so that people can momentarily catch their breath and pursue ways of personal renewal. It's the need to stay in balance!

This need is claiming the attention of an increasing number of executives. There's more to life than work. There are personal relationships to be nourished into blossoming flowers. There's an intellect to be challenged, creativity to be unleashed. If one wants to have a reserve from which to make a contribution, there's also the need to find some way to be spiritually renewed.

The need for balance has raised new opportunities and issues. It's a significant part of the genesis behind such recent workplace innovations as company-provided day care, flex time, family leave time, parent in-service training, video- and teleconferencing, and virtual offices—some of which may be considered critical factors by those candidates being interviewed.

Remain professionally competent

"I know that one of the first things I have to do when I start my new job is to learn a couple of new information systems. I also need to master our proprietary software. I've got a steep learning curve ahead.

"My biggest concern, though, is what else is going on that I need to know but will be too busy to learn."

In today's exploding marketplace there's so much to learn and so little time, that the expertise one acquires can be absolutely critical for a particular task at hand while being absolutely irrelevant for any other position. Choosing what is essential to know

for one's current position—and for one's future professional viability—has never been more difficult.

This much, however, is certain. In addition to
technical knowledge, emotional intelligence has
become extremely critical for success. In an effort
to hit quarterly numbers, a Catch 22 is created by
many organizations when decision makers reduce
training opportunities. Justified by short-term
longevity, they fear little immediate ROI on such
expenditures even though funding for the development of human resources is essential to remain
competitive.

There's validity in that conclusion. Organizational pass-through time has been shortened. Executives keep looking for new ways to put notches on
their belt of experience.

> "I'm going to give it my all," said one vice
> president the day before he began his new job. "I
> know this. It's a start-up and I think they're
> preparing to build it up and then sell it off. I'm not
> sure how long a run it will be but at least I'll add
> one more credential to my resume."

Executive candidates who are personally committed to being on the cutting edge want to know how
your organization will support their development.
In today's marketplace, it's a critical piece of information to factor in to their response.

Benefit financially from her or his ability

Although today's successful executives appreciate security, they're increasingly more entrepreneurial and willing to risk. Often, their primary emphasis is not on salary or bonuses but on stock options. That's how they can keep score of their contribution to the success of the business.

> "I guess I'm a gambler at heart," said one COO. "I already have some security so now I'm ready to roll the dice on this new venture.

> "We've got a good team assembled. I think I've done my homework and that my assessment is correct. We've got a great product. The challenge is to booome a brand.

> "I think I can help us get there and they've made it attractive. Salary isn't nearly as high as my last one was, but I've got a great option package and I'm vested an additional 20 percent each year.

> "If our projections are anywhere near correct, if I decided to cash in and do something else, in even three years I'll walk away with several million. That's a lot more exciting to me than working for a larger salary and bonus."

▲▼▲▼

Entering into a partnership relationship is not just a one-way street. It's certainly important to know what you need. It's just as important, however, to take seriously the needs of your potential partners. Always, there's your side *and* their perspective.

No partnership relation-

ship can exist with your

new executive if your

way always prevails!

PART IV
Support Success

CHAPTER 19

Select The Best

The bumper sticker read: *My daughter is an honor student at Green Tree Junior High.*

As if in response, another bumper sticker read: *My child is an average student and I'm proud.*

However stated—defensively or tongue in cheek— the question is, how acceptable is average?

In days of yore, being considered "average" was not usually viewed as an impediment to success as long as one showed a strong work ethic and respect for others. With today's need for having and managing knowledge, however, just being average isn't enough.

If your organization is to capture and maintain a competitive position, you've got to select executives who possess the necessary aptitudes and attitudes to quickly "fit in" and contribute.

> "We've got some new executives in our top slots," said one chief operating officer, reflecting on recent appointments. "They seem to be nice people and they're bright—but some are having a tough time getting any traction. They just don't seem to have what it takes to adapt to our way of doing things. That's really costing us and we've got to get a better grip.
>
> "We're putting people in high-profile positions and then hoping. But it's not working. We're wasting time and energy, and we're missing opportunities while they're having a tough time assimilating. With a big lag time before they make an impact, there's no way we can be competitive. We need people who can quickly adapt and immediately begin working with us, but we're not finding them."

Today's constantly churning marketplace has heightened the need to select executives who possess qualities of excellence—and that's not going to happen by hoping. If you're going to hire right, you've got to improve your selection process!

Selection considerations

Achieving outstanding results while working for another organization doesn't guarantee that someone will be able to produce as well for yours. There are too many variables. That's why determining the best person for *your* organization is loaded with potential for failure.

When decisions are shaped by what's been done in the past, defining prior experience leads the search effort. Frequently a minimum number of years is desired. You might focus that requirement even more narrowly to include only industry-specific experience.

Such requests have been useful in former days. However, the demands of today's rapidly evolving marketplace create a need to act differently. For businesses poised on a misty knoll of uncertainty yet seeking firmer footing, experience forged on the anvil of a different era has become irrelevant. Relying on that experience may not even be *helpful.*

In prior times, people enjoyed the luxury of gradual acclimation. Others expected their learning curve to stretch over several months. That's no longer tolerable. There just isn't time.

"If she can't come in with a bang, know exactly where she's going and how she intends to get there, take charge, and get some quick hits within her first four to six weeks—she'll never survive.

"There's no time to waste. The rules are to get a
quick start or get out of the game," commented
one corporate officer. "It may not be what we'd like
it to be and it may not be fair but that's the reality.
She is either prepared or not. We don't have time
to wait while she flounders."

The window of opportunity for hiring the best executive for your organization has narrowed. At the
same time, the challenges have increased. To identify a candidate who will be able to contribute immediately to your critical success factors, you must
commit time to a careful diagnosis of the broad
spectrum of the required technical, interpersonal,
and team aptitudes and attitudes. Refusing to recognize that reality—and accept it—will make it
prohibitive for you to hire for fit.

Watch out for halos!

Like any courtship, interviewing will always have
its subjective moments. Allowing these to become
distractions that dominate your selection, however,
is a recipe for disaster. After you've made the
commitment and invested the time to develop a
customer-responsive position description, it's best
to stick with it. Otherwise, it's easy to make well-
intended but poor choices based on "gut feelings."

At times, internal candidates who are well liked

and skilled at what they do appear. They have received positive acclaim and likely deserve a promotion. Particularly if you already have a good working relationship with them, it's tempting to overlook their "flat" sides. It's easy to be lulled into a quick decision that remains untouched by your customer-responsive position description.

Sometimes, an external candidate quickly makes a favorable impression. A cursory review is made of highly commendable references and the interviewing process subtly shifts into an attempt to "sell" the position to the promising candidate. It's easy to forget the critical task of selecting the candidate who best fits what's needed.

"I was really impressed with her," the COO commented. "She made such a positive impression on me, I felt very comfortable during the interview. It was more like a conversation.

"I concluded that she would be great to work with—and her references backed that up. So I made her an offer. I didn't think it would hurt that she would be the first woman at this high a level in our organization."

"She's been here three months and she's already demonstrated a couple of things. First, she's a hard worker. Second, she sure knows how to rub people the wrong way. She does it without realizing it. And she does it so often, she's isolated herself.

"The halo of what I thought she represented blinded me and I made a poor selection."

Do your due diligence

Never overlook the due diligence process. Wordsmithing can produce a polished résumé that impressively hits critical key words. Individuals can prepare themselves to be very smooth in their interviews—and that's particularly true when those conducting the final interviews for the corporation do it so poorly.

"I hate interviewing," said one president. "I'm far from skilled at it. I really don't know how to probe deeply so I leave that part to others."

Line officers, especially at senior levels, rarely interview—but when they do, much is at stake. Knowing how to determine the choice pick has costly implications. That's why stumbling through the process is intolerable.

Sharpened selection processes equip those conducting interviews to use:

- Customer-responsive position descriptions

- Scenarios

- Consistent templates

- Reference research

Customer-responsive position descriptions

Appropriately forged, customer-responsive position descriptions define the technical, interpersonal, and team skills required for a "fit." They form the basis for hiring individuals who will contribute to the success of your organization. When this step is bypassed, organizations unintentionally set themselves up for costly transitions.

> "Our top team, including me, have all come on board within the last ten months," commented one vice president of human resources. "We're reorganizing, everything is changing, and we've got a long list of vacancies.

> "Being busy isn't the same as being focused. We've got to take time to figure out where we're headed and what's needed to get us there—and it's more than technical skills."

Scenarios

It's true that most line managers have only a passing knowledge of interviewing techniques. That's why they frequently ask closed-ended questions and dabble in superficial subjects.

They need help—most of them desperately. One effective approach is to craft scenarios that reflect "real-time" issues. With those in hand (and, remember, they can be developed by anyone familiar with how the organization really works), even senior executives can listen carefully to what is said (and what is not said) in response. With this method, they gain much greater insight into a candidate's ability to fit their specific needs.

Consistent templates

When used effectively, consistent templates can assure much greater objectivity in hiring. Designed to apply criteria evenly, they can be used to list, prioritize, and rank the perceived technical, interpersonal, and team capabilities of each candidate.

Research references

Any candidate can and will provide you with some great references. Because they select who can tell you about their abilities, their references are guaranteed to be exactly as they want them to be. If you want to identify those who will best fit within your organization, push beyond their initial offering of references.

> "I've found," said one HR vice president, "that if I take a couple of additional steps at a referenced company, I sometimes find very helpful information that's waiting to be revealed.

> "I first interview the references provided. Then I ask for names of two or three other persons who have worked with the candidate.

> "When I follow through, I take the same action with those people. I find that provides me with a much more complete picture."

▲▼▲▼

Selecting the best executives for your organization requires a commitment to objective decision making guided by a customer-responsive position description. It also means you've got to avoid halos—worn either by the executive candidate or by you.

On rare occasions dumb luck may work—but there is no guaranteed shortcut to hiring executives who will contribute to your organization's success.

20

Supporting Start-Ups

"It's a great opportunity with plenty of challenges," she said. "I just hope I'm up to them.

"I want to contribute, to add value—but to really be able to do that, I've got to get up to speed on several things.

"I need to get a better understanding of this company—what its critical success factors are and how they work. I'm committed to doing that— I just hope I have enough time."

Even when your candidate has been carefully screened, meeting those success factors is easier said than done.

A person entering a new position can quickly get overwhelmed. Everyone has expectations and makes demands. Reacting to each demand—often in an unfocused way—causes time to fly by rapidly. It also tempts your new executive to use "busyness" as an instinctive excuse to stray from mission guidance control and from mastering the specific nuances of her or his new organization. Despite the best of intentions, it's easy for failure to follow.

The overlooked opportunity

Most organizational leaders are at least subliminally aware of the possibility of missing an opportunity for success at the time of a new executive's entry. They become frustrated when it takes too long for that person to get rolling. That's why they frequently use some sort of orientation program to introduce individuals to their new challenges.

Often the orientation consists of little more than a friendly welcome, presentation of an employee handbook, a review of benefits, and some cursory introductions. With that minimal effort, the "newly hireds" are considered launched into the organization and are then expected to make it on their own.

"It was a quick swirl," she said. "A once over lightly and I was left to sink or swim on my own.

"After more than two months, I'm still trying to get clear about a lot of things. It's like I've been asked to jump on a train already speeding ninety miles an hour. I can hear the whistle, but I'm still trying to find the tracks."

In my experience, the higher the position, the less the emphasis on getting "newly hireds" carefully positioned so they can make an immediate contribution.

"We've got to do a better job of helping people get started," said one division president six months into his new position. "I've been fumbling my way through trying to find someone who can tell me how to get things done and getting a handle on key operating issues. I've been making mistakes and wasting time. That shouldn't be happening to me or to anyone else."

Failure to use the entry opportunity—to help someone understand your organization's focus, be clear about what specific contributions they are expected to make, and recognize how the success of others depends on their activities—undercuts the potential contribution your new executives can make. It restricts their quick-start capability and leaves them unfocused. As they attempt to right themselves, it can also incur needless expenses while, with the best of intentions, they chase irrelevancies.

Remember this: the greater the role clarity, the greater the opportunity for both individuals and your organization to flourish. Don't overlook it!

Stuck on assumptions

When pointed out, this missed orientation opportunity becomes obvious. Just being aware of it, however, will not necessarily have any impact on organizational behavior. Frequently, assumptions have a much firmer grip.

When I asked the president of a major pharmaceutical producer what his company does to help new executives get started, he responded very directly.

> "We take a 'cave person' approach," he said. "We throw them into the situation and hope they survive. Sometimes they build hills they have to climb. Sometimes it takes longer than we want for them to get up and running. Sometimes they don't make it. Then we have no choice. We get a replacement.

> "Besides," he continued, "I don't see that as our responsibility. We're paying people enough so they ought to be able to get started without any help. If they can't, then we've undoubtedly made a wrong choice."

That's a common and a very erroneous conclusion—and it has the potential of huge costs for your organization. It can easily play into a dangerous assumption. And your new executives are likely acting on that same assumption.

To demonstrate both competence and confidence as they enter into a new position, many executives feel reluctant to ask for help. That's not to suggest they don't *need* help—or even that their need isn't recognized. Many times, they acquiesce to the prevailing thought that they should be competent enough to make it on their own and couple that with the questionable conclusion that to *not* know everything is to be vulnerable.

That assumption is inaccurate. People aren't vulnerable because they don't know everything. They're vulnerable when they act as if they know, then proceed full speed ahead. They're vulnerable when they conclude, "I'd rather do it myself," instead of choosing to benefit from other people's experience.

If entering executives are to succeed, their peers must push aside assumptions that create gridlock. Their initiatives will be far more effective if the organization readily makes available information that is both critical and useable.

It's clarity that's needed!

For any initial entry or ongoing activity to be productive, you and your organization need to deliver to the candidate accurate answers to at least these four critical questions:

- What are we trying to accomplish?

- What are our critical success factors?

- What are we expecting our new executive to contribute?

- What's the culture within which our new executive is to get results?

What are we trying to accomplish?

Until pressed, people act as if they share a common understanding of the responsibility confronting them. When questioned in depth, however, a variety of different perspectives often surface.

> "I have to continually remind my team members," commented one chief executive officer, "that the real enemy is out there, not in here. They've got to stay focused on the same objective. Frequently that doesn't happen."

"I think what I've got," said another chief executive officer who had just entered that position, "is a group of fiefdom heads each pulling in separate directions."

The tug-and-pull behavior of well-intentioned but unfocused executives wastes time, money, and energy. It happens because individuals, acting in haste, assume they have a shared understanding of what needs to be accomplished. Rarely is that true. If your new executive is to contribute to your organization's success, she or he must be clearly focused. Take the time and expend the effort to describe the results you expect. And restate a common focus over and over and over again. To let new executives stumble toward their own discoveries is to court disaster and jeopardize success.

What are our critical success factors?

It's possible to be extremely busy while accomplishing little. That's why focus is so critical. Focus should include more than a generalized statement of the end goal. It should also include specific results to be achieved along the way.

Those results should also include a description of how individuals are expected to work together, and they should be measurable. How else will you know what has actually been achieved? How else will the guideposts to what's critical for your success be identified, met, and celebrated?

> "I sometimes wonder what I'm accomplishing or if I'm getting done what needs to be done," said one CIO three months into her new position. "I know I'm busy reacting to demands and pursuing my own game plan—but am I putting my efforts where the company wants them put?
>
> "No one is telling me I'm not—but it's a nagging question. I can't seem to get any clear answers. I need some way to chart my progress in addressing what's critical. But so far I haven't found that way."

How are we expecting our new executive to contribute?

Everyone has expectations, but unless they are articulated, your new executive has little likelihood of meeting them. After all, you can't expect him or her to be a mind reader.

Depending on how others relate to the position held by your new executive, expectations will differ. Often they are not prioritized. Rarely are they stated.

"I'm trying to get my own stuff done," said one vice president of sales. "That's enough of a challenge—but it seems like everyone else also has their demands.

"If this company is going to be successful, I have to deliver for them—but I'm still not sure exactly what they need, or when. It would help if this wasn't a matter of guesswork."

To hope newly hired executives will be able to correctly read and appropriately respond to a multitude of unexpressed expectations in a timely manner is to set them up to fail. Be very clear about all the expectations you have of them, recognize a necessary prioritization must occur, and make certain you have carefully discussed these priorities. That's a contribution *you* need to make to leverage your orientation efforts for success.

What's the culture within which our new executive is to get results?

No two organizations are the same. Indeed, no two subparts of a single organization are identical. Each has its own history, values, priorities, and ways of making decisions. Each also has its own centers of influence that differ from any depiction on an organizational chart. This informal environment has the ability to adversely impact a new executive's success potential.

Appearances can be deceiving. So take time to describe the context for getting results, then interview and hire to its parameters. Most important, make that context visible. Only then can your new executive have the information needed to make an immediate and meaningful contribution to your organization's success.

> "I knew it would be a challenge," one CFO said as he left his new organization in less than six months. "I thought I had enough experience and savvy to get on top of things.
>
> "What I thought I saw wasn't what I got. I've been blindsided so many times. It's like I kept trying to figure out how I could get the job done while responding to management by whim."

One more consideration

Star athletes, opera divas, superb instrumentalists, and prima ballerinas consistently use coaches to help them extend their performance. Each recognizes that there are always nuances to master in order to achieve and retain world-class status.

Unfortunately, the executive mind-set frequently acts on a different assumption. Giving lip service to continuous improvement, many present a model that suggests "what's worked in the past is sufficient for the present as well as the future." As a result, the ability to be on the competitive edge of individual as well as organizational performance is drastically diminished.

The fast-paced change of today's marketplace highlights the fallacy of depending on "repeat performance." Organizations are gradually recognizing the critical need for mentors or coaches—but applying such a label does not a developer of executives make.

If you are committed to assisting your high-potential, newly selected executives in leveraging themselves as a resource, you will be well advised to encourage them through word, example, and financial investment to obtain coaching that can help them stretch. Make certain, however, you select a coach that's right. The right one will provide them with valid, descriptive, non-judgmental operational feedback and will support them as they risk extending and polishing their interpersonal and team skills.

▲▼▲▼

The successful assimilation of a new executive into your organization will never just "happen"—nor will it be accomplished by magic. It will require hard work that may extend several leagues beyond your usual orientation efforts. Set aside assumptions. Establish specific focus. Put measurements in place. Minimize surprises.

Success results from a partnership effort in which each person knows specifically what he or she must contribute!

The *ROI* of New Eyes

Sometimes I've looked in my closet for a particular suit, shirt, or tie and couldn't find it. It's not that it wasn't there. Someone else could plainly see it—but at the moment, I couldn't.

The obvious isn't always apparent. I can look and not see, and I suspect I'm not the only one. At times like that, I appreciate having another set of eyes to help me find things I am missing. That's valuable.

Executives new to your organization can add similar value as they experience how it functions. They can, and undoubtedly will, raise questions about how you've become accustomed to working.

"I just don't understand why they do things the way they do," said one vice president of sales. "I've only been here for a little while and I'm certain I've got a lot to learn, but some things just don't make sense.

"I ask questions but no one seems able to answer them. Things are done a particular way because they've always been done that way. That's the total rationale I get."

What does Clarence think?

I worked with a CEO who wanted a quick start in his new organization. Its founder had been an old school "hammer manager" who, totally committed to his dream, had done whatever it took to create success. When he died, the business was grossing $55 million.

Selected to institute more contemporary management practices while continuing to grow the business, the new CEO faced many challenges.

Initially he took a low profile, listening carefully and occasionally raising questions to test the waters.

"I've been thinking about . . . what do you think?"

"What would happen if we. . . . ?"

"Have we ever tried . . . ?"

The response he received became predictable. Inevitably, the discussion led to asking, "What does Clarence think?" (Clarence, he quickly learned, was a long-standing employee who supervised less than half of the production lines in the plant.) Yet members of the workforce, particularly old-timers, always asked that question. So did most members of the board of directors.

Clarence's opinion counted and, on first blush, the impact of his influence made little sense. As a line supervisor, he held no key management position in the company. But whenever a new possibility affecting the entire company was raised, so was the too-familiar question,

"What does Clarence think?"

Learning the background provided some insight. Years earlier, Clarence had been the first individual hired by the founder. Every morning for more than thirty years, the two sat down for coffee and shared a single bagel. As they ate breakfast, they dreamed and planned for the future. The business grew beyond Clarence, but the morning routine never varied. Because the founder kept using him as a sounding board, it was easy to understand why everyone would ask, "What does Clarence think?"

Originally it may have made sense to listen to Clarence's opinion. It was an understandable response, appropriate for the moment. But like many activities, this had become habitual—and the habit stayed long after it had validity.

That's true in most organizations. Haunted by the ghost of their own "Clarences," leaders can automatically follow questionable routines that have become ruts—forgetting that depth is the only difference between a rut and a grave.

Listening to questions raised by a new executive can provide new opportunities to see some benefit if certain activities were handled differently.

Knee-jerk resistance

Whenever anyone questions their actions, people often automatically respond with resistance. That's understandable! Effective or efficient or not, it's easy to become accustomed to certain behavior patterns. They are more comfortable than trying something different. Because they disturb a sense of how things "should be," questions can disrupt a sense of security and raise resistance.

> "I just don't understand what she's trying to accomplish," said one mid-level manager about his new COO.

"We used to know how things were to be done. For no apparent reason she's questioning all sorts of things and expecting us to do things differently. I just don't like the way things are going and neither does anyone else."

Face it! Few executives are brought into your organization to maintain the status quo. They are expected to bring and use the gift of fresh perspective, to raise questions, and to introduce change—*but only to a point!* Resistance will usually surface to temper and limit the impact of that which is proposed.

Resistance has many faces. It can be overt or covert. It can be perceived as a problem or a challenge. It can be displayed through coercive attempts to put others down so that one's own feeling of importance might be highlighted. Individuals in resistance frequently grumble as they gather around the communal coffeepot. As a result, they squander much time and effort.

Introducing a new executive into your organization will inevitably trigger such responses. Those responses must be managed! Throughout their professional careers, most executives may have had change "done" to them and they may have "done" change to others. Few, however, have had the opportunity to be trained to be an agent of change.

If you want to support the success of your newly hired executive, you must be aware of the minefield that person's introduction into the company will create. You want new executives to impact the situation. They want to respond. But don't make the assumption they will have all the necessary skills. Few will.

To be successful, they're apt to need a mentor or coach who has appropriate change agent experience. It may be someone within your human resources department. It may be another line or staff officer. Or it may be important to reach out to a third-party mentor who has the experience to objectively provide both focus and feedback.

Your new executive brings the gift of fresh perspective and can provide insight that will help everyone contribute more to your organization's success.

It's a limited gift!

Few gifts last forever. Certainly the gift of a new perspective does not. The first thirty days are critical. During that time, your organization is a wonderland waiting to be discovered. Questions are inevitable. Soon, however, enthusiasm wanes and routines cloud the vision.

That's why, if you want to take advantage of the gift, your pre-search homework becomes crucial.

Before you ever conduct an interview, you need to answer these questions:

- To what extent will we intentionally invite our new executive to look carefully at our practices?

- What forum will we provide for her or him to raise questions?

- How willing are we to be open to questions that challenge the way we've become accustomed to working?

- What are the routines and practices that are not to be challenged?

- Ideas for change introduced by a fresh view create opportunities. Like any gift, they can be unwrapped and used. They can also be thrust aside.

▲▼▲▼

My wife searched to find a very special holiday gift for our four-year-old granddaughter. Finally she found a doll that we both just knew she would like. But the morning our granddaughter opened it, she spoke with the bluntness of innocence. "I don't like it," she declared. That was that. She would have nothing to do with the doll.

The gift of fresh insight offered by your new executives can also engender such a response. You may not like what they have to say. Yet resisting that gift can erode your organization's ability to use current opportunities to build on past successes.

After one gift is ignored,

the next gift is more

reluctantly offered!

CHAPTER 2

"Fit" Doesn't Mean More of the Same

Birds of a feather flock together. Of course they do, for a variety of reasons—even in organizational life. Commonality is comfortable. Common bonds are helpful. Differences that need to be managed tend, at least on the surface, to be few.

Perceived realities often influence the selection of executives. The same kind of industry experience—having worked with someone in a former company, school ties, the "old boys' network"—

can contribute to a quick, although perhaps superficial, rapport and lead to a favorable nudge.

> "Of all the individuals I interviewed, I really like him the best," commented one COO.

> "He's just like us. He thinks like us. He seems to be comfortable with us. He's worked with some of the same companies I have—even knows several of the same people I do."

That's one way of hiring—and as understandable as it is, it also raises questions. In today's environment, it's impossible to be all-knowing. It's a key reason why uniformity of leadership thought and action isn't all that helpful. It can even lead to failure.

Success requires a diversity of experience and expertise. It requires individuals who approach challenges differently and who see options and opportunities that others do not. It also benefits from varied approaches to the management of tasks and people.

How valid is it, then, to permit your selection of a new executive to be guided by asking, "How much *more* of what we already have does our candidate bring?" Would it not be more helpful to ask, "What different perspectives does he or she bring that can add value to our efforts?"

Differences make a difference!

Entrepreneurs love the chase, the thrill of the hunt. They know how to identify possibilities that emerge out of uncertainty. Often acting alone, they can surface an endless list of new targets to be pursued while leaving the more traditionally minded exhausted. They thrive on action and on getting results—until the hunt is over. Then, they're immediately on to the next challenge.

They simply don't like the details in which some seem to delight. Details, of course, are critical when it comes to matters financial, strategic, and tactical. They make a difference when it comes to research, quality control, and production schedules. But except for wanting to know they are available, most entrepreneurs prefer to ignore them.

> "My CFO is driving me crazy," said one CEO, evaluating his recently inherited staff. "Larry brings me a report that goes on for pages and he wants to review it with me.
>
> "He's well meaning and he's a stickler for details. That's why I need him. The details—they're critical—but don't bother me with them unless I ask. I have a few numbers I regularly track. Give me a one-page summary and no more than two pages of questions and answers about the report. If I need more, I'll ask."

Many managers are shaped by such a drive. They analyze quickly, make a surface pass at separating the wheat from the chaff, and usually make a decision on the spot. It enables them to make strong contributions—but realize what chaos would reign if their approach to details permeated their entire organization.

Also needed are those who dig more deeply as they take an analytical approach and acknowledge that established parameters exist for a reason. Not all limits are restricting. Most need not be. Setting them aside should, however, be intentional with full awareness of the ripple effect that each such action will precipitate.

Both those who can't wait to rise to the next challenge and those committed to work within the organization's parameters make their diverse contributions to your organization. So do those constantly focused on accomplishing the task as well as those who recognize that completing it without strengthening relationships will contribute to failure.

Appreciate the positive difference differences can make. Use that insight to select individuals who provide the diversity that will strengthen your organization's success potential—and provide them the support they need.

Relationship bridges are critical

Your new executives are more apt to be working with

others than in isolation—and not everyone will share their worldview. If you're fortunate, in fact, they will approach things quite differently from you. They'll hear what they want to hear. So will you. When it's not the same, it can be exasperating and even cause breakdowns in communication.

For example, if you tend to approach subjects like an entrepreneur, you are apt to look for opportunities, be viewed as competent, and exercise power. That's why language that speaks about challenges and risks—the opportunity to achieve, to take action and get results—can be far more exciting to you than a drone of details.

Others, however, may prefer the details. Being right is important to them. They do not easily embrace challenges and risks. They want certainty and consistency. Their antennae are most receptive to language that defines limits and focuses on quality and correctness. That's the kind of information *they* need to be successful.

Some executives will focus strictly on getting the task accomplished. For them, it's a matter of doing whatever it takes to get the job done. Others will recognize the need to maintain a balance between task and people concerns. They'll want everyone to be involved, to have a strong sense of worth, and to intentionally develop relationships. They're more ready to hear language that underscores values and includes others in shaping the situation.

Each of the above circumstances can be both an instinctive and a learned way of operating. It's never a matter of being right or wrong. Each can be appropriate or inappropriate for a given situation. Each can be a strength and—as is true with any strength—when taken to excess, it can certainly become a weakness.

To support the success of your new executives, learn to use language they are ready to hear. That's how you can replace assumptions that lead to misunderstandings and begin to build bridges of communication that equip working relationships for success.

Answer before asked

> "I'm really trying to get hold of this new job," said one COO, "but I'll be honest. I feel like I've been abandoned. My CEO has been on the run since I started and I just can't get time with him.

> "I've got questions and I want to make sure we build a good relationship."

Questions inevitably come up for those entering a new position. The answers can provide a rudder to help them navigate toward success. Many questions you can anticipate. If you provide answers before these questions are asked, you will make a major contribution to their success.

How do you prefer to manage?

Some prefer a short leash. Others want a long one. Some want daily reports, with details. Others want a periodic verbal overview. Some expect those who work for them to take great initiative. Others demand, even at the highest levels, to approve every action.

The CEO of one major financial corporation insists that even though it's an approved budget item, he must personally sign any expenditure over $5,000—and at least see any that will cost more than $500.

It's important for your new executive to know how *you* prefer to work. It's better to be clear than to be surprised—and perhaps upset—when, even with the best of intentions, they don't meet your unexpressed expectations.

What critical success factors guide your actions?

One of your new executive's responsibilities is to help you succeed. What are the factors by which your success is measured? What specific contributions do you require from those who work with you? What else do others need to accomplish and within what time frame if they are to measure up to your expectations for their success? Don't assume they know. Remember that you undoubtedly see things from a different perspective than they do.

Bringing focus to your expectations is likely to be difficult. It frequently has been for me. When I was a CEO, one of my greatest challenges was to quit expressing myself in a general way and get results-specific. I'll admit it wasn't easy. However, if I took the time to become precise (and realistic), those who worked for me were always more focused, more responsive, and more productive. Most important, their efforts were always more pleasing to me.

How will you make yourself accessible?

In today's highly transitory work climate, it's difficult to get together. Executives are always on the go, traveling, working in different time zones, and using teleconferencing as a medium of communication with others.

There's still a need, however, for people to be in greater touch than can be provided by e-mail. Especially in their initial ninety days, new executives need to be able to reach out to you—for background information and for your guidance.

How will you make yourself available to them? Will they be expected to send messages by phone, fax, or e-mail into a black hole of oblivion while they wait for your reply? Or, will they receive a prompt response from you? When will you commit the time to meet with them? How much time will you make available? How often?

▲▼▲▼

Similarities cluster together. Too many similarities, however, will contribute to failure. If you want your new executives to succeed, look for and value the differences they bring. Manage those differences by providing a focus that produces positive results.

Managing differences well can be an essential ability needed to leverage your potential for success!

23

Action:
The Mother
of Results

In my youth, I learned a wonderful lesson when someone pointed out to me the big difference between wanting a field to be plowed and plowing it. One is a wish; the other requires a commitment to take action. That difference is what transforms desire into reality!

Throughout my life, I've wanted several things. Little happened, however, until I took appropriate action. Just wanting something didn't make it happen.

You may sincerely want the person you select for a position in your company to succeed. That's why you may be in the process of clarifying and strengthening your support of new executives. Such thinking provides an excellent starting point—but it's not enough. If you want them to leverage their unique talents and their gifts of fresh insight, you also have to provide them with the *authority to act* and the *financial resources to implement actions*. Far too frequently, that doesn't happen.

The regrettable truth

I never cease to be amazed by the number of executives—even those at or near the top—who accept a new position, begin planning for what needs to be done, and yet have absolutely no idea what authority or budget they have to support their initiatives.

> "Of course we aren't making any money," said one newly landed COO, "but we've got $5 million in start-up funding.
>
> "We've got to use it wisely, but who's to determine how we target its use? There's no budget. No one knows what each department has to spend. How do we work out our differences—or do we? We're running so fast we don't have time to talk about these things."

One NASDAQ corporation had been experiencing a 20 percent annual growth rate for three consecutive years, with no let-up in sight. The board chairman and president finally concluded it might be helpful to establish an HR function. They searched. They interviewed. They hired.

The successful candidate was given the title of vice president. He was also given this mandate:

> "Do whatever it takes to help our people manage the chaos created by our growth. Just let me know what you need," said the president, "and I'll make sure you get it."

The first day this new VP was on the job, the corporate counsel dropped by his office. After welcoming him on board, he proceeded to pass on some information.

> "Our president," he said, "has decided his plate is too full for you to report to him so you'll report to me. Just let me know what you want to do—what training programs you think are needed, what kind of consultants you want, anything like that. I'll let you know if we have the money."

Would it surprise you to learn that some initiatives the HR vice president thought were absolutely essential to carry out the presidential mandate were not considered worth funding by the corporate counsel?

Avoid lost opportunities

Frustration builds and countless opportunities are lost whenever people are expected to produce but have unworkable limits—either authority or budget—placed on them. Sometimes the setup is inadvertent.

A new executive inherits a spending plan shaped by the priorities and values of her or his predecessor. Conditions change and perspectives shift—especially when it takes some time to fill the slot. Being bound to an inherited budget immediately blunts one's ability to take advantage of opportunities.

That's not what you want. It's not what your new executive needs personally. It's about having clear, honest answers to your new executive's questions:

- How flexible is the budget I have inherited?

- What funds are available to support the initiatives I identify?

- How free am I to spend these funds?

- Who are the people I must convince before I can tap into them?

- What if the approvers don't agree?

- What impact will these limitations have on my ability to be successful?

An appropriately chosen new executive can make a major contribution to your organization if you're committed to support him or her. Trust your selection process enough to value her or his new insights, then provide the resources that new person needs to make a positive impact.

When interviewing, encourage discussion about a separate start-up budget to implement initiatives spawned by the new executives' fresh perspectives. This budget could include purchasing new equipment, training teams for competition in today's changing marketplace, coaching for themselves and their direct reports, and much more. Expect accountability for this budget. And don't force them to go through any hoops to spend it.

Trust your selection process, trust your chosen candidate, then support his or her ability to add to your success.

A lesson from my past

My first day in university, I was among a group of freshmen taken on an orientation walk to familiarize us with the campus. One of our first stops was old alumni hall. Its red brick showed signs of wear. Its granite steps had been hollowed by the footsteps of nearly a century of students.

As we entered the hall, our own footsteps echoed off hard surfaces and high ceilings. Through a door off the entrance area, we were led down a rickety set of stairs that would never have passed an OSHA inspection. Light filtered through three small basement windows curtained by years of dust. At each end and midway on each side, a heavy electric cord led to a lighted forty-watt bulb at the end.

Gradually our eyes adjusted. In the dimness, we could see a vacant spot where the old coal-burning furnace once stood. It had provided heat to the few buildings on a young campus. Some old coal bins remained and so did the acrid smell of coal dust.

"What do you see that seems unusual?'" asked our guide.

Thankfully, I didn't blurt out my first reaction by saying that everything seemed unusual.

But bit by bit, we noticed that countless chips of wood had been knocked out across the top of the coal bins, on their corners and even on their side planks. Some chips even had chips of their own.

"Now," said our guide, "for the rest of the story. Many years ago, two students wanted to learn how to hit a baseball in a different way. Every day throughout an entire academic year, they came down here and practiced. In fair or foul weather— even when it was stifling hot from the furnace— they would practice, practice, and practice some more. As they did, the baseball would chip away at the wood of the coal bins.

"Those students continued to perfect their skills as they learned how to lay down a bunt. Eventually they went on to play professional baseball. Today you'll find both of them—Hugie Jennings and John 'Mugsy' McGraw—honored in the Baseball Hall of Fame at Cooperstown."

The young athletes knew what they wanted, but they had to refine it, to polish it, to develop it into a skill. It took a commitment to devote the necessary time. It took persistence and effort that translated a concept into a personal capability.

"As you go through your classes here," our guide continued, "you'll be introduced to new ideas and possibilities. Being exposed to them, however, doesn't mean you'll be able to benefit from them.

"You'll have to work with them. Polish them until they become a part of you. Then you, too, will be prepared to succeed."

▲▼▲▼

Throughout this book you've been given much information. Some you may have already known. Once it was pointed out, some of it may have seemed quite obvious. Some of it may have introduced you to new facets for consideration.

Just because you've been exposed to these ideas or insights, though, doesn't mean you're now ready to benefit from them. *Wanting* to use this information simply isn't enough. *You've got to do it!* Hone it against your experience. Practice until it becomes instinctive. That's what will equip you to select the best and hire for fit.

If at first you don't succeed, question your actions, learn from your answers, then try, try again!

THE
PRODUCTIVE
ENTRANCE
STRATEGY®

CHAPTER

24

A Resource
For Success

When there's so much to do and so little time, a vacancy adds to the workload of others and can easily tempt those responsible for filling it to hurry through the process.

Yielding to that temptation, however, sows the seeds for potential failure. *Remember, on average, within eighteen to twenty-four months, 40 percent of all executives entering into a new position will fail.* At higher levels, costs of such failure can run up to 24 times base salary—and sometimes, even more.

Resources of time, energy, and goodwill will be squandered. Opportunities will be missed.

THE PRODUCTIVE ENTRANCE STRATEGY®
is a resource that requires a collaborative effort
among all significant customers of the position to
be filled. It will lead you through a process that
may seem far more detailed than others you know.
That's probably because it is. As a refining
process, however, it minimizes your risk, helps you
hire for fit, and supports the success of those
whom you select.

THE PRODUCTIVE ENTRANCE STRATEGY®
consists of the following steps, explained throughout the book and summarized in this chapter:

- Clarify background information

- Review fit factors

- Develop a selection template

- Assign to search

- Structure interviews

- Implement entrance strategy support

Clarify background information

Since no position exists in a vacuum, it's important
to see it in context. Each position serves a diversi-

fied number of customers with its own sets of needs. Each also exists to contribute to meeting organizational issues.

Answering the following questions will help you develop a customer-responsive position description that takes context, customers, and contributions into account:

1. Who are the different customers served by the position?

2. What specific goods or services is the position expected to deliver to each?

3. What is our corporate mission?

4. In what way is our mission used as a lens through which to view operational and strategic opportunities—including position vacancies?

5. To what extent is our vacant position description an *accurate* representation of what we really need to implement our mission?

6. What assumptions are we making about the spectrum of skills required to fill the vacancy?

7. How precise have we been in describing the

specific functional/technical skills required (they're different) to implement our mission?

Review fit factors

Executives rarely fail because they lack necessary technical skills. Far more often, it's because they lack interpersonal and/or team capabilities to succeed within the realities and nuances of a particular organization.

In developing a customer-responsive position description, commit yourself to carefully reviewing the following fit factors:

- Alignment

- Culture

- Expectations

- Change

Alignment—The First Fit Factor

This factor identifies the specific contribution to be made by the person in the position to meet organizational objectives. You will be well served if, before rushing to search, you invest your effort in answering these questions:

1. What changes are taking place in our marketplace?

2. To what extent are these changes impacting our ability to carry out our stated mission?

3. To what extent should our mission be redefined or modified?

4. What actions are critical if we are to achieve our mission?

5. What objectives must the selected executive meet if she or he is to contribute to the implementation of our mission?

6. What time frame have we set for accomplishing those objectives?

7. To what extent does our position description list activities to be performed *or* accomplishments to be achieved?

8. What commitments are needed from others in our organization to support the accomplishment of those objectives?

9. What skills—functional, interpersonal, and team—must our new executive possess if she or he is to significantly contribute to meeting our objectives?

Culture—The Second Fit Factor

Before rushing to search, invest your efforts in answering these questions to describe your work environment:

1. What behaviors do our leaders champion by deed as well as word?

2. In what way are we responsive to our customers?

3. What gets in the way of our workflow?

4. How do we address bottlenecks?

5. What personal contributions are given public recognition?

6. To what extent is the recognition we give positive, negative, or nonexistent?

7. What's the relationship between our reward system and the productivity of individuals and/or teams?

8. To what extent is our definition of productivity "qualitative" as well as "quantitative"?

9. How do we celebrate our achievements?

10. To what extent do we invest in the development of each of our employees so they can assist us in being competitive?

11. Who will be responsible for describing the environment into which our new executive will be entering?

12. What skills—functional, interpersonal, and team—must our new executive possess if she or he is to work within our culture and contribute to our corporate success?

Expectations—The Third Fit Factor

Through experience, you know that expectations must be known before they have any chance of being met. That's why critical expectations should be clarified and prioritized before you can incorporate the aptitudes required into your search. Ask these questions to determine your and your organization's expectations:

1. What were the strengths of our previous position holder?

2. What are the critical success factors of each of the position's customers?

3. What must those customers get from the selected candidate if they are to be successful?

4. How do we want our new executive to manage others?

5. How do we want her or him to resolve differences?

6. What role do we want our new executive to take in developing people?

7. What possible difficulties could be encountered working with peers?

8. How do we want our new executive to keep us informed?

9. How do we want *bad news* presented?

10. To what limits is our new executive to adhere?

11. How do the expectations of various position customers differ?

12. What steps are needed to prioritize diverse expectations?

13. What skills—technical, interpersonal, and team—must our new executive possess if she or he is to meet our expectations?

Change—The Fourth Fit Factor

It's important to assess the challenges of change confronting your organization and to clarify—rather than assume—what skills you need your candidate to command. Before you begin your search, answer these questions:

1. What changes are taking place in our marketplace?

2. How are those changes impacting our primary competitors?

3. Where do they have a competitive advantage?

4. Where are they most vulnerable?

5. What's our competitive advantage?

6. What opportunities are current marketplace changes providing for us?

7. What's our strategy for meeting that challenge?

8. How realistic is the timetable we've set?

9. How will these changes impact the way we do business?

10. What resistance do we anticipate?

11. What internal/external resources do we currently have in place to support the implementation of our proposed change?

12. How do these realities shape what the executive we select needs to accomplish and within what time frames?

13. What skills—technical, interpersonal, and team—must our new executive possess if she or he is to successfully lead our change initiative?

Develop a selection template

You're never going to get every aptitude and attitude you would like to have when you select your new executive. Still, you need to assess the range of technical, interpersonal, and team skills that would best meet your vacant position's diverse customer needs. Then, sort them into capabilities critical to your organization's success and the skills you would also like to have.

Review those skills you've identified in your background information and fit factors review. Reach as much consensus as you can among customers. Then use this form to prioritize what you need:

Must have	**Would like**

Technical skills

1 _____ _____

2 _____ _____

3 _____ _____

Interpersonal skills

1 _____ _____

2 _____ _____

3 _____ _____

Team skills

1 _____ _____

2 _____ _____

3 _____ _____

Only at this point are you properly prepared to go to search!

Assign to search

There's an abundance of potential candidates in the marketplace. However, only a select few may have the technical, interpersonal, and team skills as well as the attitude appropriate to fitting into and succeeding in your organization. Most will not. That's why it's so critical to take the time necessary to clarify *exactly* what target you are pursuing. Once that's defined, your search efforts will be much more precise, will waste less time, and will provide both recruiters and your human resource staff with a template to screen out all but the most appropriate candidates.

After this initial screening, it's time for the customers of the position to conduct a series of interviews.

Structure interviews

Multiple interviews are the norm. Being intentional with them can gather more useful information than can unplanned conversations treated as part of the screening process. Remember, your objective is to

eliminate all but the best candidates. That winnow-
ing process should be conducted against a consistent
template of those capabilities you must and would
like to have. It's the only way you can position yourself to make appropriate comparisons that will help
you select the best person to fill your vacancy.

Use these questions to structure your interviewing process:

1. Which customers will participate in interviewing your candidate?

2. Who will orient those responsible for interviewing and manage the interviewing process
   to ensure that it proceeds in a smooth and
   timely manner?

3. What scenarios and/or data-gathering questions will be used to gather information?

4. Who will develop the interviewing questions
   and scenarios?

5. Which customer is expected to raise which
   questions?

6. Who will be responsible for probing for additional information about attitudes and aptitudes?

Implement entrance strategy support

Even if you've followed **THE PRODUCTIVE ENTRANCE STRATEGY®** exactly as it's been outlined and have made your selection, don't assume your new executives will automatically be successful. They won't! They need a support structure to enable them to make the best contribution possible. You have a responsibility to make certain one is in place and operable. Use the following questions as a checklist to make certain you've at least covered the basics. These will help new executives get a quick and productive start:

1. Who will mentor your new executive through the first ninety days?

2. Who will review organizational culture, procedures, and the diversity of customer expectations with her or him?

3. What plans have been made to establish (rather than assume) a positive working relationship with the person to whom your new executive will report?

4. What is expected of your new executive in a direct reporting relationship?

5. What accessibility (frequency and availability) will your new executive have to the person who manages him or her?

6. What budget does your new executive have to manage?

7. What spending limitations are expected?

8. What start-up budget has been established for your new executive to spend, without approval, to address necessary initiatives?

A Final Word

Every executive replacement creates an opportunity to leverage your organization's potential for success—but there's nothing automatic about that possibility. You need to identify the position's customers and design a screening template of technical, interpersonal, and team skills to effectively meet the needs of those customers.

It's critical to develop a rudder that helps you consistently navigate the challenges of selection. This book is your rudder. It will help you minimize the potential for drifting into an unintended collusion to fail. It will keep you from squandering valuable resources—time, finances, and goodwill.

And it will keep you from letting opportunities slip by unnoticed.

Hire for Fit describes the process that will position you for the task. It's not an easy one. It will require more focus on your selection initiatives. It will consume time out of your already busy schedule. But if your objective is to select someone who fits your organization and support her or his success—there's no other way. Use this book and, specifically, **THE PRODUCTIVE ENTRANCE STRATEGY®** to take you through a step-by-step process that *ensures* you hire for the best fit and *encourages* you to support the success of the person selected.

▲▼▲▼

Thank you for the opportunity to share this resource. I welcome questions about how I can assist you as you pursue this process. For sharing your time with me—thanks!

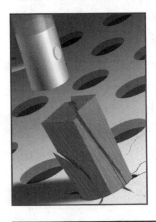

Hire people who fit your organization and support their success!

About the Author

Don Andersson is a nationally recognized executive resource, speaker, and storyteller who provides out-of-the-box thinking and pragmatic insight that helps corporate and association leaders who want to leverage their human capital assets.

Through presentations, seminars, executive and team coaching, Don Andersson helps senior executives increase individual and team effectiveness. In anticipation of search, he often works with them to develop a customer-responsive position description. After selection—through team development initiatives—he works with organizations to support the success of the choice they have. *Please note:* Don does not do the search!

Don Andersson is frequently quoted by the media and thirty-five hundred chief financial officers worldwide read his column, "Ask the Transition Coach." Author of several articles that have appeared in national and industry specific magazines, he is also the developer of **THE PRODUCTIVE ENTRANCE STRATEGY**®, and two audio albums, "Streamline Your Transition" and "Take Charge of Your Entry." *Hire for Fit* is Don's first book.

Former CEO of a $500 million public sector corporation, Don has a background in strategic planning, marketing, executive, and organizational development. He has been a consultant to the Center for Management Development at Rutgers University, a visiting professor at New York University, and an adjunct professor in The Graduate School of Business at Fairleigh Dickinson University and Wagner College. He is also a member of the National Speakers Association.

For further information about the resources that Don can provide for you, please contact Don@AnderssonGroup.com or 888-709-9267.

Don Andersson
The Andersson Group
7 Pittsfield Street
Cranford, New Jersey 07016
908.709.9267
Don@AnderssonGroup.com
www.AnderssonGroup.com

INDEX

A

Amelio, Gilbert F., 28
Andersson, Don, 235–36
Apple Computer, Inc., 28
AT&T, 23, 28

B

bad hiring decisions, costs of, 27–32
Borders Group, 24

C

career transition costs, 2

D

Di Romualdo, Robert, 24

E

employer/employee loyalty, 121
entrepreneurs, 211
executive retention, 124–26
executive search ranges, 152–54

N

O

P